Spirit-Led Sobriety

By Paulette Kengg

Spirit-Led Sobriety

by Paulette Kengg

International Standard Book Number 978-0-9906219-8-0

Scripture quotations in this book are from the NEW AMERICAN STANDARD BIBLE, ®, Copyright © 1960, 1962, 1963, 1968, 1971, 1972, 1973, 1975, 1977, 1975, 1995 by The Lockman Foundation. Used by permission.

Neither the publisher nor the author is engaged in rendering professional advice or services. The ideas, procedures, treatments and suggestions in this book are not intended as a substitute for consulting with a physician or therapist. If you're considering quitting alcohol, consult your physician before doing so. Some individuals have had seizures that may lead to sudden death if they quit without the help of a qualified healthcare professional, hospital or treatment center. Neither the author nor the publisher is liable or responsible for any loss or damage allegedly arising from any information or suggestions contained in this book.

Names of individuals, as well as minor details, have been changed for privacy.

Dedication:

I dedicate this book to God, Who rocks my world like no other.

To my dearly-loved, greatly missed parents. How I wish the help available today was available to you both, back then. I have no doubt you both did the best you could with the limited resources you had at the time.

To my siblings. How grateful I am we've come through our childhoods and each ended up quite nicely. God is good.

To my beloved husband, daughter and grandkids. How blessed I am to be a part of your lives.

To my treasured friends, friends I have had for 25+ years (in alphabetical order-LOL): Pat B., Cathy B., Delynn B., Deb N., Sherri T. and Stella Z. What a beautiful family of friends you are to me.

To Annie Grace, Mark Shaw and countless others whose work has helped me along the way.

Last but not least, to my fellow Himalayans. What a path we've been on together.

And do not get drunk with wine, for that is dissipation, but be filled with the Spirit.—
Ephesians 5:18

Taken from the *Merriam-Webster Dictionary*:

Spirit

<u>Noun</u>

<u>Synonyms of spirit</u>

... a supernatural being or essence, such as capitalized: Holy Spirit

... <u>distillate sense, such as</u> (1) the liquid containing ethanol and water that is distilled from an alcoholic liquid or mash

- Often used in plural
- A usually volatile organic solvent (such as an alcohol, ester or hydrocarbon)

Neuroplasticity

<u>Noun</u>

... The capacity of the brain to develop and change throughout life, something Western science once thought impossible.

lovely humour to balance it. It is certainly NOT a dry book as a result (pun not intended there)!—Nicola Foster, Edinburg, Scotland"

"I could not put the book down. It's an insightful and deeply-felt narrative of a true caregiver with a strong faith and love of the Lord. I was blessed enough to be in the same online program group with the author, as we found freedom from the grasp of alcohol and the ability to forgive ourselves and grow in many areas of our lives through Annie Grace's program. She is so open in sharing her struggles and successes in the support group and in her book. Your story may be different, but you will find her story, resources and passion to share helpful in your journey to a joyful life."—Marie Thomas

"I experienced an emotional roller coaster while reading this book, which is exactly what I strive for whenever I crack open a new novel. When the author related her tales of tragedy and victory, I was captivated. She grew in her faith as she learned to rely on God to lead her, frequently stepping out in faith when she had no idea where it would go.

"I could identify with her as she gave alcohol a purpose/role in her life and altered her relationship with it. But eventually, she was able to break free from alcohol, as may all of us, and this book can help others find this lovely freedom. It combines her tale with God's inspiration and serves as a reliable reference manual.

"If I could pick one Bible verse to encapsulate *Spirit-Led Sobriety*, it would be this: Isaiah 61:3 "To all who mourn in Israel, he will give a crown of beauty for ashes, a joyous blessing instead of mourning, festive praise instead of despair." This book is a lovely representation of beauty for ashes."—Carolyn Bennett, TNM Certified Senior Coach with The Zero Proof Life

"Very interesting and edifying. The topic is totally on target!"—Pastor Victor J.

"As the son of a father killed by alcohol abuse I am grateful for this book. The author has a pastor's heart and gifting. She demonstrated her concern for the downtrodden in a previous book, and now turns her passionate concern to those trapped in an alcohol-dominated lifestyle."—Anonymous

"It's with the help of this author that I was encouraged to write *Godly Women Waiting for Godlly Men*. I had no idea she was facing such a battle as this. I am humbled and honored to add my voice to her new book. This book is informative, well-written and offers so much information, both spiritually and practically, in the world I have always known as "alcoholism." In this book, she bares her very soul to us, knowing that it will be easy to judge and even condemn her. That's brave. I winced. I groaned. I cried. What a battle she fought and will continue to fight. But I know her. God is #1 in her life and with His grace and mercy and that of her family and friends, "the battle is already won."—Honey Gilmer, Author

"Brave and inspiring! Opens your mind to the truth about alcohol. Gives hope to the hopeless." —Mandi Hendry

Contents

Introduction:

It's no secret that the enemy of our souls, a/k/a Satan, seeks every possible opportunity to take us out, spiritually-speaking. The last thing he wants Christians doing is drawing closer to and obeying God, fulfilling their purposes in doing what He's called us to do.

One of the many ways—perhaps the most destructive way thus far—Satan has come after me was through normalizing the use of alcohol in my eyes as a child, deceiving me into believing it was something good, tempting me with false promises of stability, security, confidence, love, healing, entertainment and so much more. And then laughing for decades as I took the bait, over and over and over again.

Perhaps you're like I used to be. You've been drinking alcohol for years, as a "normal drinker", and suddenly you realize you're drinking way more than you ever intended, far more often than you ever intended, and for reasons you never intended.

You're both terrified and confused because you can't understand what's happened, and why you can't seem to stop and 'stay-stopped', no matter how hard you try. You sincerely want to quit drinking, and wake up every morning proclaiming there's no way you're drinking again after last night ... only to later in the day be triggered like Pavlov's dog hearing the bell, you find yourself drinking again. Take heart, loved ones.

Even the apostle Paul was guilty of the same thing (Romans 7:20-25). From a worldly, mental health-based perspective, he suffered from cognitive dissonance. *Merriam-Webster's Dictionary* defines cognitive dissonance as a "psychological conflict resulting from incongruous beliefs and attitudes held simultaneously".

I call it 'hell on earth, psychological warfare, torture,' all of which create unimaginable feelings of guilt, shame, and for me worst of all, self-loathing.

As you begin reading this book, you will notice I share information from a spiritual perspective as well as that based on science-based research and studies. There is nothing wrong with science in of itself, as God is the

Creator of all things—including science. We need the truth of God and evidence-based research and facts based on scientific studies to understand what the world refers to as 'alcoholism', 'addiction' and 'alcohol use disorder' (AUD), all of which you will find here.

Be sure to check out Chapter 10—Resources, where you'll discover that alcohol doesn't discriminate. You will learn that pastors, a Catholic nun, an author from a large, well-known Christian publishing house, an attorney, college professors, a well-known CEO and businessman, etc. have also developed and recovered from addiction and AUD. I'll never forget the relief I felt when—after summoning the courage to call one of my pastor friends from church to admit my problem—he immediately said to me, "I have been clean and sober for well over 20 years."

People with AUD or who have become addicted to alcohol are not moral failures. More often than not, I would venture to say there's someone in your own life who may be fighting this internal battle but is too frightened by a fear of rejection, as I did for years. Maybe, it is you.

The stigma of the drunk on the street corner has GO TO GO. With alcohol being the legal, affordable and highly promoted street drug that it is, I fail to understand why it's a surprise to anyone when they or someone they love discovers they're in alcohol prison.

We're all sinners saved by grace, so why is it people who develop problems with alcohol are made to feel as though we deserve to be burned at the stake, while those committing adultery, bribery, murder, robbery, abuse, are addicted to porn, shopping or gambling, are lying to our faces from Washington, DC, etc. are left untouched?

Judge not, lest you be judged.—Matthew 7:1

One of the reasons I wrote this book is because the one place I thought I should have been able to turn to for help—the church—was the last place I felt I could do so. Addiction and, specifically alcohol misuse, are rarely discussed in a sermon.

I believe God will use this book not only to bring hope, redemption and healing to those who read it, but also to give pastors a tool to bring the discussion before their congregations and bring things out into the light, where there is healing and no more reasons to hide.

Just like the rom-com movie from years ago starring Nicholas Cage and Bridget Fonda—yes—it can happen to you. Don't ever think it can't. And the scary truth is, no one ever knows whether or not the next drink they have, will be the one that lands THEM in alcohol prison. Your brain is not the dashboard of a car, and you will not receive a warning light.

In closing, have hope. Perhaps God led you to this book for such a time as this. He loves you, has a great plan for your life (Jeremiah 29:11-12) and stands ready to help you when you call out His name at any time.

In His service and yours,

Paulette

Chapter 1

I Should Have Died

MAN, my back is KILLING ME. Why can't I move? What is WRONG with me?

I lose consciousness again, not realizing at the time that I'm losing blood. All over our beautiful hardwood floors right between the family room and hallway of our beloved lake front vacation condo. Alone for the next four days while my sweet husband is at a business conference hours away.

MAN, my back is KILLING ME. WHY? And WHY is our leather sofa so WET? I need to go to the bathroom. I need some Advil. God, I need help getting off this couch.

God hears me and helps me get off the couch and to the bathroom. I flip the switch in the bathroom to see why my back is hurting in a way that can't possibly be described.

WHY can't I SEE anything? WHY are my GLASSES BROKEN?

Turning my body to the side, I see through very poor vision with my own eyes that blood is pouring out of me on the left side of my back, in an area that my right hand can't easily reach. Not good, considering I can't see well, and I'm right-handed. I put on every Band-Aid I can find, because that's all I can do, as I need to get back to the couch because I'm SO TIRED.

I was so tired, I guess because I was losing so much blood. Not being trained in healthcare, I can only guess this is the reason. I can't think of doing anything else but slowly making my way to the couch, where I slowly lie down and lose consciousness again, my brain trying to save my life by doing so.

SHUT UP, you stupid pelicans! GO BACK TO BED, you stupid sun! I'm not ready to see you, I need darkness because I'm SO TIRED. And, my back is KILLING ME. WHY is the couch so wet? What is that gross smell?

With what can only be described as angelic strength, somehow—SOME how—I'm able to get off the couch. I can't help but reach towards the area where my back is searing with pain, only to discover in horror, that for some reason, large Band-Aids I don't remember putting on, are slipping off because my blood is pulsing out of me with every movement.

WHY am I SO DIZZY? I have got to get to the bathroom and get some more Band-Aids. WHY are my GLASSES BROKEN?

In the bathroom, I get a hand cloth to stop the bleeding, because there are no more Band-Aids. One thing I know for sure, I have got to get to the clinic in town as soon as possible.

You may be thinking at this point, "Uhm, call 911! Call Preston [my husband]! Call Betty [the condo property manager] to drive you because your glasses are broken!" I can't tell you why these thoughts never occurred to me—but they didn't. I pray for safety as I drive the long, winding and hilly road for the 10 minutes it takes to get there, in so much pain I can't even cry.

In what can only be described as a miracle in my opinion, if you knew how freaking blind I'm without my glasses, if you could have any comprehension—ANY, of understanding of how much pain I was in, or see the amount of blood soaking into whatever I was wearing (I can't remember)—I arrive safely, walk gingerly to the counter and sign in.

"Reason for Your Visit?" they ask. *I'm in intense pain, I hurt myself and I'm bleeding, people.*

I'm fairly certain at least an hour goes by before they call me into the room where the doctor treats patients, because by this time I have sobered up enough to monitor this sort of thing. The nurse comes in, asks the usual questions, and after asking me to lift my shirt, immediately opens the door and yells for the doctor. She finds a clean cloth, towel or something (I can't remember) to press into the wound site to stop the bleeding.

An ambulance is called. Several staff rush into the room. Questions coming at me like flying bullets, my head hurts and after bandaging the wound as best as they can, I'm furious that they refuse to let me lie down because (I guess) at this point, I have lost so much blood they fear I may lose consciousness and never see my family again.

SHUT UP! MY HEAD HURTS! I'M TIRED! WHAT KIND of people ARE YOU?

"Stay with us. You've to stay awake. Where is your husband? Where is your cell phone? We need to call him," one of them says.

OH GOD, NO! OH GOD, NO! OH GOD, NO! PLEASE-PLEASE, PLEASE, PLEASE, LET ME JUST DIE. I don't want Preston to know I'm hurt! I don't want him to know I drank whiskey AND took an Ambien so I could be SURE I fell asleep last night! GOD, I will never—EVER—ask for anything else I promise, if You would please just let me die. You don't even have to let me into Heaven. I know I don't deserve to be in Heaven. I'm sorry. Please God, I'm begging you. Please let me die now, so I don't have to see Preston's utter disappointment in me.

I'm scared he will divorce me right away. Samantha will hate me too, and may never let me see Chace and Jack [my grandkids] again. I know for SURE, my siblings will never talk to me again. Either that, or they'll talk alright and I'll <u>never</u> hear the end of this horrible mistake, how stupid I was, how they don't blame Preston and Samantha for a *half a minute for washing their hands of me, and how I'm 'on your own now, find your own place to live because you're sure not living with me'.*

The ambulance arrives, and when they lay me on the gurney, I think that is when I stopped talking to God and started begging them to let me stand up now, because I only THOUGHT I wanted to lie down. I'm crying, begging them to stop talking *please stop asking me so many questions I don't care if I'm supposed to stay awake you don't realize how exhausted I'm why the HELL won't you give me anything for pain what kind of people ARE you I thought you're paid to help people feel better I'M DYING WITH PAIN, GIVE ME SOMETHING GIVE ME 100 INJECTIONS OF SOMETHING!*

They keep talking. At this point I remember thinking they are lying to me when they tell me we are almost at the hospital, to "hang on." I want to close my ears with my hands when they tell me they have called Preston and he's on his way, but at this point, everything hurts. Blinking my eyes, hurts. Breathing and talking, hurt. Life, hurts.

Although my physical pain was like nothing I have ever felt before, it was a day at the beach compared to the emotional anguish and fear of how much this was probably scaring my beloved Preston, the sweetest and kindest man I have ever known this side of heaven, who didn't deserve a wretch like me for a wife.

We arrived in the ER where they began doing their thing, all the while I'm crying and begging for something for the pain. They explained they can't do anything until they run tests to determine if I have had a traumatic brain injury. Since I have no idea at all what happened to me—none—they are doing the right thing for me, even though I don't like it. Drapes are drawn around me for privacy, as there are other patients being treated. I try to stop crying, because blowing my nose causes the puncture wound in my back to hurt even more.

And, I continue to beg God to let me die right there and even send me to hell if He wants to, because I can't bear the realization of how much I have hurt Preston. Please God, let someone in this world have mercy on me and take me in when he kicks me out of the house, until I get on my feet.

I can't remember how much time passed other than several hours, before they wheeled me out into the freaking hallway for all the world to see. I was so tired, but they wouldn't let me sleep. It's just as well because I probably couldn't have done so, even if I'd tried. Insomnia was a dragon I had been fighting for years, it began when I started what would become one of my favorite jobs.

Eventually Preston arrives, immediately takes my hand, bends down to kiss me, tells me that he loves me and asks how I'm feeling.

Like I want to die, Preston. You don't deserve me go ahead and leave I understand no one could blame you I'll sign the papers I deserve nothing therefore I ask nothing not even your forgiveness because I don't deserve that I'll be fine somehow God will take care of me because He always has go ahead and walk away now as I'm going to beg God to let me die enough now until He lets me do so.

Preston flags down one of the doctors for an update but I can't recall what was said. At some point they move me into a private room, and by this time it's late at night, I think sometime after 10 pm. My hand has been held by Preston's the entire time. There has been a shift change and two new staff members come into our room, very somber. The nurse tells me she believes I was sexually assaulted. Preston holds my hand a little tighter. The air in our lungs was sucked out like a vacuum in one fell swoop. My heart dropped to my feet, and my body felt on fire.

Based on the location of my puncture wound, how deep it was, my bruises, my broken glasses and the fact that I can't remember anything, she believes I was sexually assaulted and asks permission to conduct a SANE test. For anyone reading this, SANE stands for "sexual assault nurse examination".

I don't remember if I mentioned to her that I was raped the night of my 19th birthday while a virgin, and that I remember every vivid detail including how scared I was and how much it hurt, but if I didn't, I should have. Because I had no pain "down there", and when a woman is raped, let me tell you, it hurts a GREAT DEAL, "down there". For many days.

Preston and I are shell-shocked by this information, and he encourages me to say 'yes' but ultimately it is my decision. I do so only because I will do anything for this beautiful man who I can't believe is still by my side holding my hand and lovingly stroking my arm. He's asked to leave the room, I begin to cry, which only hurts all the more.

Many questions are asked, humiliating things are performed on and to me, pictures taken—not something I would wish upon anyone.

After they leave, Preston, a police detective and one of the nurses return to the room. The detective asks if it is OK if I answer some questions, to which I agree to in spite of my fear. I let him know in advance that I don't know how much help I will be, given I remembered nothing.

He's very kind, expressing compassion and saying he's very sorry this happened. As he does so, all I can think of is how I honestly don't believe that it did, because I don't hurt "down there". There are no bruises "down there" and there would have been if my legs had been forced apart without my permission. These are details, a woman never forgets for the rest of her life.

Once he's finished, the detective explains that he and Preston need to go to the condo immediately to gather evidence and take photos, and that the nurses will be in to check on me regularly. Preston bends down and kisses me, strokes my face softly and says he would not leave me but he must do so, he would be back as soon as possible, and to call him on his cell phone if I needed him.

I lie there alone in the dark, in the worst physical and emotional pain I have ever been in my life, realizing that I'm going to live after all because I deserve to suffer for the rest of my life. I deserve what's coming, which of course will be divorce, homelessness, never being loved like I was by anyone ever again, never seeing my daughter or grandkids again. In my mind I'm planning which homeless shelter to go to first.

I stare at the ceiling, frightened out of my mind, and as much as I try not to cry because doing so only increases the pain, I do so. They have given me something for pain, finally. I want Preston, but I can't talk to him right now because he's driving with the detective, so I call the only other man I want to talk to: Henry, my big brother.

I tell him where I'm and what I'm told happened to me, because I didn't remember anything. I lived to regret this phone call, as all it did was lead to undue pain, worry and fear for everyone in our family. Preston and I were told by healthcare professionals and police detectives that I was sexually assaulted, and since I didn't remember anything, we believed them.

Eventually I'm released and wheeled out to the car with a pain Rx already filled, where Preston had already reclined the seat as far back as it will go so I will be as comfortable as possible for the long ride home. We ride primarily in solitude, except for when he so sweetly asks me if I'm OK, do I need my pillow adjusted, is there anything he can do for me and tells me he's so glad I'm alive and that everything will be OK.

I don't remember what time we finally arrive home, but Preston puts me to bed, tells me he loves me and he's right there if I need anything. He lets me know that he told his boss what happened and asked him to keep it as confidential as possible, telling only those who needed to know. I have met his boss and wife before, and knew he would be trustworthy.

Please die, right now. Die. You don't deserve to live because all you do is hurt those you love. WHY can't you get your act together? You USED to NEVER have a problem with alcohol.

What happened?

Several days went by before we heard from the police detective. He and a woman detective on returned to the condo the next day after the property manager let them in, because they needed to look for evidence in daylight.

Within minutes of being there, it was the woman who figured out what more than likely happened, based on available physical evidence.

According to her, sometime in the middle of the night or wee hours of the morning, while on the way to the bathroom from the sofa, I tripped over the laptop's cable, hit my head on the corner of the wall across from it, and fell backwards.

And in doing so, impaled myself on a wrought iron spike that was one of many on an antique quilt rack, losing consciousness at this point, as the blood began pouring out my body. Similar to Indians or some fishermen today impaling fish with a spear, there I laid for who knows how long, bleeding, unconscious, and alone. My back was impaled on a wrought iron spear about three inches deep, I later learned. Bleeding profusely. I could have—and feel I should have—died right then and there. I deserved it, but God saved me for some reason— maybe, for such a time and purpose as this.

To this day, I have no idea how I was able to remove myself from it, much less anything else that night/day. My stomach turns every time I think about it.

We were relieved to know I wasn't sexually assaulted. Preston informed my family of the detective's final report, took great care of me and worked in his home office while I healed from my alcohol-induced injuries.

I was in such physical pain, taking such strong pain medicine and all I did was sleep for at least a week. I fought back tears on a daily basis—almost always unsuccessfully—wondering, *HOW did I become addicted to alcohol? And, when?* I was in my mid-50s and had never, not once, been unable to control my drinking. I was filled with great shame—as if it were some sort of weakness or moral failing on my part. That's the decades-long stigma that society has allowed for people suffering from addictions and substance use disorders. In many ways, people like me feel like lepers from the Old Testament. It's so unbelievably unkind to treat people as such.

At that moment I knew I NEEDED to quit drinking. For years I'd wanted to and exhausted myself trying, but this time was different. I HAD to do this.

You would think, after this near-death experience, I would have done so immediately. Sadly, that's not the case. I kept trying to quit and stay quit, but was never able to for years. Always trying to find a way out of hell, never realizing what the real problem was, and Who ultimately held the key.

At my age, I have no problems sharing my mistakes and stories if it will help others. I want my life to make a positive difference in the lives of others, and I want to help you end your suffering. You're not a bad person, you're a person with a bad but fixable problem with the help of One Who loves you so much.

If you're struggling for spiritual and science-based solutions to get out of alcohol prison yourself, don't give up. You don't need to go back to the proverbial "Day One" as is often done through Alcoholics Anonymous ("AA"). Now don't misunderstand me. I'm well aware that AA has helped perhaps millions of people since its inception to achieve sobriety.

God uses many things to help us in every area of life; for me, AA did more harm than good. For one thing, I never accepted their insistence that I label myself as an "alcoholic", and I never believed it was a disease. Besides, I didn't want to settle for "sobriety". I wanted—prayed for, worked hard for—freedom from this bloody nightmare, and I now have it.

Speaking of labels, why does society put the blame on individuals when it comes to AUD, the most updated diagnosis issued by National Institute on Alcohol Abuse and Alcoholism (NIAAA)—but not people addicted to cigarettes or heroin, for example? Why aren't there "cigaretteahholics" or "heroinaholics"? Why are they referred to with compassion as "people who became addicted to cigarettes and/or heroin"?

Uhm, I'm not making excuses, but have you opened your eyes to the non-stop INYOURFACE marketing by the alcohol industry? It's everywhere, people. Commercials on TV, home improvement shows, sporting attire, movies, books, videos, kitchen gadgets and glassware, its everywhere you look. Open your eyes and look around. It's so prevalent that you may not have been aware or thought about looking around for it until now.

Finding freedom from alcohol is beyond a shadow of a doubt, the hardest thing I have ever accomplished in my life. And if I can do it, anyone can. Have you considered a young toddler learning to walk? How do they actually learn? They find something to hold onto and pull themselves up. Wobble for a bit. Encouraging by the cheering on of whoever's in front of them, they take a step and fall. Now think about this.

Do they STAY down? No. It is in the continual falling, standing up, and stepping forward again, that strengthens their leg muscles and helps them become strong enough to stand up without holding onto a crutch, take those first few steps in a row, and they're off and running. Literally. With so much energy, I might add!

Stop hating yourself and thinking you're a loser. You're not a loser. Speaking only for myself, I was deceived and tempted by the devil in one of the worst possible ways. We're only human, and God knows we are but dust (Psalm 103:14).

Since we are all fearfully and wonderfully made to be as different and unique as snowflakes, the ways the Holy Spirit led me to freedom may and probably will be different than how He will lead you, based on your upbringing, personality, and possibly genetic disposition.

You will learn the many ways I tried to free myself as if I were a bear cub in a trap, before God had mercy on me, spoke truth to my inner being, gently swatted me on my bum before taking me down the exact path I needed to be on; the same path I'm on, today.

Knowing that God created me with an inquisitive, analytical mind, I also needed to learn everything I could about alcohol and addiction in general from a science-based perspective. I needed to understand how, seemingly overnight, I went from someone who was a social drinker to someone enslaved by an invisible prison I was so desperate to escape from.

I set out on a long and winding path to find the answers I was looking for. And, I found them.

When you're ready, put on your best walking shoes, take my hand, and let's start climbing your way up the mountain to freedom!

Chapter 2

Hell on Earth

My siblings and I were raised by two very unhappily-married parents, both of whom drank alcohol on a regular basis. Daddy would come home drunk almost every night. Oftentimes my mom and I would get in the car and go looking for him when it became very late and she was worried. On Saturdays I remember my brother and I having to go with him to the local beer joint, where we would sit in the car with the windows down and play while he shot the breeze and drank beer, inside. The hot summer months were the worst, when our legs would begin to sweat and blister from the seats.

When one of my siblings and/or I did something wrong and got into trouble, it was just the worst. No matter what time of day it was, unless someone confessed it was they who caused the problem, all of us had to sit straight up on the couch in the family room until Daddy got home from work. The emotional and psychological damage had only just begun.

If he had been drinking when he got home, it was truly scary. Actually, that's not true. It was already, scary. One-by-one we were sent out to the backyard, where we had to pick our "switch" (a long branch from a bush with leaves on it). If the switch wasn't big enough we had to pick another one. Then we were sent to the garage, where we had to pull our pants down while Daddy swat at our bare legs with the switches, sometimes drawing blood. And if that wasn't bad enough, if our neighborhood friends were involved with the mischief, they would be peering in through the garage door windows, watching it all go down.

How many times, in the wee hours of the morning, did someone call our nearby uncle, who faithfully picked us up and brought us into his home to spend the night when Mother and Daddy got in a fight? The overwhelming shame and embarrassment I felt at having my cousins woken up—again to sleep in their bed with them, I remember to this day.

Every summer my mom would take us to spend two weeks with our favorite aunt, uncle and cousins. They were always the happiest and best two weeks of the year; that is, until we came home to learn Mother had gotten into a truly horrific car accident. Again. How many times did we visit her in the hospital, seeing her all battered and bruised, her arms and legs in very scary-looking medical devices known back then as 'traction'?

Family gatherings with our other aunts, uncles and cousins were always loads of fun, and except for one couple, they all drank. Loads.

As we grew older, our parents became increasingly unhappy. Eventually they separated and I was devastated, because Daddy was my world. Of my two parents, Daddy was the one who loved me, told me he loved me, was affectionate and gave me confidence. I don't write this from a victim-mentality, by the way, but more matter-of-fact, as is my nature.

Being the youngest of many kids, after FINALLY producing a son, the last thing Mother wanted or needed was another child to deal with.

Enter me, into the world. Looking back, I don't blame her for having a hard time developing any feelings other than disdain for me. The poor woman was stuck in an abusive marriage with too many kids in too small a house; and, especially back then, well, you just didn't talk about these sorts of things with anyone.

Thankfully my childhood wasn't a total 365 day per year nightmare, and my siblings and I do have some good memories. But for the purposes of this book, I'm focusing on the experiences that shaped me the most, and to shine a light on how far I have come since then.

For whatever reason, I was either born with bad hearing or developed bad hearing as a young girl. I was deaf in one ear, wore hearing aids and went through numerous painful surgeries. When Daddy left Mother and us for a trial separation, I remember laying on their bed crying my eyes out and blaming myself because "I" was costing them so much money. Thankfully, although I don't remember who it was, someone eventually came in and comforted me when I told them why I was crying my heart out.

I had no way of knowing at the time, but in spite of everything, my parents were determined to work things out. Daddy was in rehab off and on, and I remember having to go to Al-Anon meetings and visiting him in the hospital at least once.

One night on one of my sister's birthdays, when I was only 14 years old, he came over to see us. Our parents were flirting with each other like mad, and we had never seen them so happy. Their reconciliation was announced, and he was moving home the next morning. We were all just ecstatic, especially me. Within minutes of this huge announcement, the doorbell rang and I realized it was time for me to leave for my babysitting job.

The following morning I was vacuuming in the living room, getting ready for Daddy's homecoming. The doorbell rang, and a very solemn aunt stood on the porch, asking if she could come in, and if there was anyone else at home. I called my sisters from upstairs. Mother was—I guess—at the grocery store, and I don't remember where my brother was.

"Your daddy's dead," she said.

I went back into the living room and started vacuuming because I wanted the house to be clean when he came home. I remember hearing my sisters screaming, and being angry and confused with myself, shaming myself for not crying. As a young girl, I had no idea I was experiencing shock and denial.

The technology and possibly DNA-research tools available today were not available decades ago when this life-changing event happened. We learned the police were called to grandma's house hours after one of our uncles, who had been drinking, shot our dad, based on the coroner's report. Apparently Daddy laid on the floor of his closet bleeding to death while the murderer called their other brother, who may have told him 'don't call the police, we need to figure out what to tell them.'

This was my first experience with how alcohol can ruin lives, not only of the person drinking it but those around them.

I don't know <u>for sure</u> this is what transpired; I only know the death certificate listed suicide on it, and this is what I was told. Not only was this significant for my family and I on an emotional level, it severely impacted our lives from a practical standpoint. Life insurance companies don't pay out to the surviving spouse if suicide is listed as cause of death.

Our poor mother, heartbroken I'm sure, that she and her husband had finally worked things out and realizing he was NEVER coming home again. There was no way she could support my siblings and I on her meager secretarial income without taking drastic measures. She sold the larger, much nicer home they purchased a year before this happened, and bought a fixer-upper in a great part of town. Joanna Gaines hasn't got a thing on our mom, she invented the white kitchen!

A few days later my best friend and her sister invited me to spend the night and go see our favorite musician at a local small live concert venue. They plied me with plenty of beer on the way. Alcohol was introduced to me by my peers as a way to relax.

Like literally all of my friends in high school, I drank quite a bit on the weekends. There was no supervision, and everyone was doing it. It was nothing to drink beer at 10 am on the way to the beach. My friends and their sisters were older than me, and I felt stupid if I didn't go along with them. Peer pressure is a real pain, but then you know this by now.

Ladies night at the local bars were a cinch to get into even though we were underage, and we drank and danced our fool heads off. We had some good times back then. Oftentimes I wondered how I arrived safely back home, not remembering how I got there with myself behind the wheel. Years later, I would come to learn these were called blackouts.

One-by-one my siblings flew the coop as soon as they found a way to do so, and I was left at home alone with Drunk Mother. I was out drinking almost every night so I wouldn't have to deal with her. God love her, she did the best she could with what she learned and experienced, growing up. Her father left she, her mother and older sister when she was quite young. Just up and left without any explanation or forwarding address. That had to have done a number on them all.

After graduating from high school, I went to college in the fall. My first true love and high school sweetheart attended a university about four hours away, and it was quite hard on me to be separated from him. Within a few months of my 19th birthday, a fellow (and quite handsome) classmate started pursuing me, and sadly I let myself get caught, primarily out of loneliness.

Studmuffin was full of testosterone and wanted only one thing, which I continuously refused to give him. Raised in a spiritual denomination that thrives on making you feel nothing but guilt and shame, my thoughts were if I refused the ultimate act of intimacy with my true love, I <u>certainly</u> wasn't going to give that part of myself away to someone I hardly knew, no matter how close in proximity and good-looking he was.

How special I felt, the night of my 19th birthday, when I walked into the apartment I shared with three other girls, to discover he organized a surprise party for me. The booze was everywhere, the music loud, we all danced and partied the night away and had a blast. Until suddenly the next thing I knew, he was on top of me in a darkened room, somehow my jeans were off, he was pulling my panties down and telling me how much I was going to 'love it'.

Suffice it to say, I knew what it was like to be drunk, but that night was very different. While I'll never know for certain, I believe he put a pill of some sort in one of my drinks. I had never felt that way before from drinking, and I have never felt that way, ever since.

Whether he did or didn't is irrelevant, because the fact is I'm the one who drank and continued to drink all night long. I remember an intense burning, 'splitting apart' pain, and asked him if we were "doing it". When a young woman has never had sexual relations before, she doesn't what to expect. He laughed and kept on proving what a stallion he was. I told him to stop, I SCREAMED for him to stop, I tried pushing him off, but he was much stronger than me. I tried calling out for help, only to be laughed at more and told no one else was there. There was no reason for him to put his hand over my mouth. No one was coming to save me.

The following morning I could barely look at myself in the mirror because of the guilt, shame and dirtiness I felt. Like any woman who's been sexually assaulted against her will, I couldn't stay in the shower long enough to feel clean. When my best friend and roommate came in from class and saw me, I felt like I'd committed murder, the guilt was so intense. I kept wondering if she could tell I was no longer a virgin.

I broke up with my first love within days because of what happened that night, breaking his heart and mine in the process. He drove all the way to see me in person to convince me otherwise, but I was in no way, shape or form, good enough for him after this. I didn't tell him— or anyone else, for that matter—what had happened, I just explained that I didn't love him anymore, lying like a sheet the whole time.

Weeks went by and one afternoon after class I went to this guy's apartment, as he and his roommates never locked the door. I continued to date him in spite of what happened, because I believed he cared for me since he still paid attention to me. Yes, my self-esteem was that low.

When he didn't answer when I called out his name, I walked upstairs and into his bedroom only to discover him 'going to town' with another girl. He turned his head, saw me—see him—smiled, turned his head back and humped away.

It was at this point I checked myself into the university clinic, crying and telling them only that I didn't feel good, and didn't know what was wrong. I was there for about three weeks, contemplating what to do next. The thought of staying in school made me sick, because not only did he live in the same apartment complex, he was in many of my classes as well. So, the only thing I could think to do was quit school and move back home to Drunk Mother. What a choice.

I continued to keep silent about the real reason why I left school, and told everyone I was just a homebody and didn't like being so far away from friends and family. Everyone believed me for years, except one of my brothers-in-law, who picked up almost like radar that something was wrong, something was different about me. I was very close to him and when he put me on the spot, I denied it before running into the bathroom, where I could cry with the faucet running.

About 15-20 years later during a phone conversation with one of my sisters, I casually mentioned what happened to me and she was positively mortified. I had always been very close to her, but she was overseas in the military when this happened. Had she been living here, I know I would have broken down and gone to her because the pressure of keeping it inside was intense.

As I write this, more than 30 years have passed. During this time, I married the first wrong guy, gave birth to our daughter, had a miscarriage and divorced him before she was two years old. Alcohol was not anything I was even *remotely* interested in. The best gift my first husband gave me was my ability to be a mom. Years later we made peace with each other and I have been friends with him and his second wife, ever since. I have nothing but compassion for my daughter's father, because like me, you and everyone else who came from a troubled childhood and/or broken family, he did the best he could at the time without a father figure role model and a mother like his.

Several years passed before I married a second wrong guy, this one was very much not a nice man, and a lover of alcohol. Boy did I ever pay for it if I didn't agree to start drinking beer with him at 10 am on the weekends (in addition to every night of the week). From an addiction-perspective, although I drank heavily while married to him, I was a "normal drinker", meaning I never craved it on any level.

The first best gift he gave me was a word processor, back then it was the closest thing to a desktop computer available. All my life I dreamed of writing full-time for a living, and he just thought for sure I would write a best-selling novel so we could become rich. The funny thing is, when I had a truly insane idea on a way to possibly create the career change of my dreams, he laughed and scoffed in my face. This was the second best gift he ever gave, as it was the springboard to jump off whatever cliff I needed to in order to prove him wrong. More on this, to come. The final best gift was when he provided the ultimate straw that broke the camel's back by hurting my daughter. What part about messing with my kid did he not understand?

Chapter 3

God. He Changes EVERYTHING

This is my 'happy chapter', the one I'm confident will blow your mind as it continues to do mine, when I look back over how my life was before I met God, and how profoundly different it is after having done so.

Life was so grand and I was just about the happiest person on this earth. I was finally a FREE WOMAN! Working as an administrative assistant since graduating from high school, I still had my big dreams for myself. I took advantage of every opportunity I could find, or in some cases—create.

At the time, I worked for a legal firm. Every month the lawyers I worked for received a newsletter from a nationwide legal association that covered our region. One day I decided to volunteer my services as an editor, and was thrilled to have my offer accepted. Anything to get experience and credibility and maybe ONE day, land me the career change of my dreams.

I can't begin to tell you, how much fun this was for me. Who cares if I didn't get paid, I was doing something I loved and felt I was born to do. No one was more surprised than me, when a year later I was presented with a beautiful black marble award for "Outstanding Newsletter Editor." #canyoubelieve

My daughter and I continued to thrive with our humble lives and tiny apartment, and I was as grateful as a girl could be. Until one day out of the clear blue sky, I was called into my boss's office and asked to shut the door.

"Blah blah blah downsizing your job has been eliminated you've one hour to pack your belongings and turn in your key. Judy is waiting outside the door to watch you and walk you to your car," he said, making me feel like a criminal or something. #asif

I will never forget that moment as long as I live, especially when walking towards my desk and seeing the picture of my dearly beloved, then nine-year-old daughter smiling at me from her school picture. And of course, it had to be Judy, standing over me like a prison guard. It turned out many people were soon to follow the same walk-the-plank scenario as I.

There was a deep, profound shame and false sense of guilt that came over me, even though I didn't do anything wrong. As I packed my belongings, a young co-worker walked by and asked what was going down, so I told her. "Who knows? This may be one of the best things that ever happens to you!" she chirped. I wanted to harm her. Little did I know at the time, she would ever end up being right.

All I kept thinking was how wrong this was, that I had worked my freaking tail off for this company, always worked overtime, volunteered to do things on the side (including helping taking photos and writing little stories for the company's newsletter)—and to end up losing my job?

Judy eyed me like a hawk and followed me down the hall, out the building, into the parking lot and made sure to get my ID badge immediatcly after I put the box of my belongings into the car. Not even a "good luck." Where were her Southern manners, for crying out loud?

It would be a long time before I realized what may have been the real reason I lost my job. I was sexually harassed by a very drunk management-level employee at a company picnic with plenty of witnesses and it was innocently recorded on my tape recorder.

You see, another step I took to creating the career change of writing full-time for a living, was to use any and every opportunity to build my writing/editing skills. Sure, I was at the company picnic for fun like everyone else, but I had also talked the HR manager into letting me write an article for the company newsletter about the picnic, including photos.

It was the industry's annual golf tournament, where companies and suppliers met up at a local golf course, played golf and enjoyed lunch afterwards. In my unofficial capacity as press spokesperson, I drove the beer cart all over the course, stopping and "shooting the breeze" (as we say in the South) with the players. I'd get my tape recorder out, record our conversations, ask a few questions and we all had a marvelous time. While sitting at the picnic table having lunch with my colleagues, this man blurted out some things that I'll never repeat, even though I'm writing this under a pen name.

It was that disgusting.

The shame, guilt and embarrassment I experienced years earlier on the night of my 19th birthday came rushing back, and I left immediately and in tears. I took off work the following day, when one of my male colleagues called and said he would be happy to back me up in any and every way possible, and how sorry he was this happened to me. Looking back, he probably thought I would have had the sense to file a sexual harassment claim, knowing I would win.

At this point in my life, I began thinking about how much my big brother had changed. He went from doing drugs to becoming a straight-up kind of guy, and I remember him telling me about Jesus and mentioning the new church he and his wife were attending.

What did I have to lose, by visiting this church on Sunday? A few hours of my time and a bit of gas in my car. What did I have to gain by visiting this church on Sunday? Why not go and find out? So, I did.

Everything. Complete game-changer, but I had no idea what would happen when Samantha and I walked through those doors. Rebel that I am, I don't like being told what to do, so I saw where Henry and his wife were sitting, and made sure we sat in an area where we wouldn't be seen by them.

The pastor gave a message of hope and encouragement, and told me God loved me and had a good plan for my life. Although I had 12 years of parochial school and dutifully attended church twice a week because I had to, I never heard anything like this. God LOVED me? ME? By the end of the service, the pastor invited anyone who was interested to come forward up the aisle to accept His free gift of salvation, invite Him into my heart and life, and get baptized.

Now I have swallowed lots of hard whiskey straight up in my life, but never have I EVER felt such a fire literally burning in my heart as I did at that moment. Honestly I thought I would turn into a pile of ashes, were it not for the tears streaming down my face as I tremble-walked up the aisle and did just that. Immediately I felt such a burden lifted off of me, like I could breathe again, even though my outward circumstances hadn't changed. I was still a single mom of a nine-year old without a job and almost out of unemployment.

After service, trying to hurry out of church without being noticed, my brother and his wife came up to me and hugged me, congratulating me on making such an important decision, and invited us to lunch. It was then I explained my situation, and he immediately asked me to let him know what my monthly expenses were, so they could help.

And help they did, faithfully, for the next two years. I'm grateful that to this day, I can look at myself in the mirror and know without a doubt that I never asked for more than one red penny than that we absolutely needed to live on.

God Grows My Faith

A few weeks after Samantha and I visited my brother's church, located about 45 minutes away, I knew it wasn't practical for us to continue driving there because I needed to save gas for any job interviews or temporary contract positions that may come along. I really wanted to find a church closer to home to help us make new Christian friends in our area, so I chose the first church I felt led to, about 10 minutes away.

When you're receiving unemployment benefits, you know the money is not actually in your checking account for very long. In my case, as soon as I received them (along with the check I received from my brother), the bills were immediately paid. Sometimes, oftentimes, things like car repairs or unexpected medical/dental bills rose up, so the money I budgeted for food and gas, went to those more urgent needs.

It's easy to say I should have kept the money for food and gas, but if you're making this assumption, perhaps you've never had bill collectors ringing you at all hours of the day and night. And—again—I literally knew God was challenging me to prove to Him that I really meant it, when I surrendered every aspect of my life to Him, trusting He would show up.

One Sunday morning I was, as they say, 'out of gas.' Almost literally, but definitely, figuratively. I felt I was carrying the weight of the world on my shoulders and didn't know what to do, because we had very little food left in the house. We had only been attending this new church for about two weeks.

We walked into the lobby of the church. I can only assume it was the look on my face and/or the deadened posture and slow gait of an elderly woman (when in fact I was in my early 30s at the time) that drew the attention of an older woman.

This sweet lady who I had never laid eyes on in my life, walked across the lobby to me that day, gently took my elbow, looked at me in the eyes and with the most tender voice I have ever heard, asked, "Honey, what's wrong?"

Now, look. Please. Everyone knows what happens when most women are asked, 'what's wrong?' Yep, you guessed it. My face crumpled, my eyes started raining tears again, and she saw I was about to lose it in front of my girl.

Sarah asked me to wait right there, before asking permission to escort Samantha to an age-appropriate Bible study class, which she did. She quickly returned and escorted me to a private room with a closed door, Kleenex box in hand, and waited for me to share my story.

When I was finished blowing my nose for the 100th time, I immediately felt so much better because someone cared enough to ask—and listen—to me. Sarah wrote her address and phone number, and strongly insisted that Samantha and I come to her house after church, so, I said, "OK". I mean—I was in God's house—so I had no choice but to say I would, right?

Well, who DOES that? Who actually drives to a complete stranger's house after church, especially with their young child, not knowing what to expect?

A desperate, laid off single mom who, while she could have always called and asked for more money, she was determined to find out if God was really listened to her prayers. Equally important, if He could—and would—provide for her needs and that of her daughter's, in spite of her circumstances.

Samantha, of course, trusted that I, her mother, trusted these people, so she had no reason to be scared. But I sure was, because gosh, you just never know.

Dave, Sarah's husband, answered the door, introduced himself, and invited us in. Thankfully she came in right behind him, so—in we walked. I thought it totally bizarre that he handed me a couple of large paper bags and a few plastic bags, while leading us to the middle bedroom of their small, humble home.

You could have knocked me over with a feather when he opened the door, saying, "Here. Take all that you need, and don't be shy."

People. I kid you, not. Think Ikea floor-to-ceiling shelves lined up like US Army soldiers, wall-to-wall (and on all four walls). Filled with canned goods, paper goods, toiletries, cleaning supplies, snacks, breads/buns, drinks—pretty much everything you could possibly need.

Sarah and Dave explained this was a food pantry they had been running from their house for several years (even though she suffered greatly from fibromyalgia and I'm sure, probably had high medical costs).

I looked at their warm, smiling faces as they closed the door—giving me dignity and grace—as I looked at Samantha, looking up at me. Slowly we began filling up two paper bags. It was one of the hardest things as a parent I had ever done. It is one thing to receive a check in the mail, but knowing your child is watching you accept handouts from strangers, was worse.

Angels Appear—Again! Not Kidding!

One November there was a knock on the door—very unusual because my friends and family didn't live close by, and we weren't expecting anyone to come over.

Samantha was home all week for the holidays, and I was feeling quite sad one evening because I hadn't had a call for an interview in weeks or even months, or so it felt.

I looked through the peep hole and saw all these teenagers standing there with a woman, all holding something (although I couldn't tell what). Cautiously unlocking the door knob (but leaving the chain intact), I heard, "Surprise! Happy early Thanksgiving! We have some things for you to make Thanksgiving dinner!"

Well, blow me down! I opened the door and in walked a parade of young people followed from behind by the woman, ordering them to put the things in the kitchen. Y'all—there was a full frozen turkey, yams, beets, rolls, green beans, brown sugar, honey, canned pumpkin and whipping cream.

I didn't KNOW these people! I had no idea how they knew who I was, or what my situation was. You would have to be a mom, to understand how much this meant to me. While I know "food is food", it meant everything to prepare a full-blown Thanksgiving meal with all the trimmings for my daughter. Anything for a sense of normalcy. Talk about being grateful.

Obviously I thanked them and as soon as they left, I squealed to Samantha like a stuck pig myself, "Samantha! Come and SEE how God is taking CARE OF US!" #bestthanksgivingever

Everything That Could Go Wrong, Did

One winter during this first layoff, I received an opportunity to interview for an editorial position in Kansas City, MO. It was an incredibly long drive to make alone, but I was so grateful to finally have something to look forward to; and, a change of scenery.

My interview was at 9 am, and when I went outside to head over to the company, I had never seen so much snow in all of my life. In fact, come to think of it, I don't ever recall having seen snow at all (since we lived in the South). Never mind that my shoes and ankles were freezing cold, I was on a mission to score a freaking job.

At least, until much to my utter horror, I realized the rent car wouldn't start. For real. After at least five or six tries.

I ran—walked carefully, rather—back into the hotel room, literally got on my knees and dialed a big 911 to God. If I didn't need His help so badly, I would have gotten pretty angry at Him.

You see—I knew no one in the state of Missouri. It was my first time there, and I have rarely felt as alone as I did that day.

"Get the phone book out and call the first church you see," I sensed Him saying. So, I did.

The church secretary answered the phone, I explained the situation and she put me on hold for less than a minute. "The pastor and associate pastor are on their way over. He asked me to tell you not to worry about anything, and that he arranged for a tow truck and notified the mechanic he used," she said.

Sure enough, they arrived within minutes. One of them took me to my interview and asked me to call him after it was over, so he could take me to the car repair shop. The other guy rode with the tow truck driver.

By the skin of my teeth, I made it to the interview on time and was quite grateful to be such an early bird who naturally wakes up with the chickens. Although I didn't want this job, I would have taken it, even if it meant pulling Samantha out of school and relocating. You do what you have to do in this life.

We arrived at the car repair shop, where I was met with a friendly "hello" and a car repair bill of $478, which I didn't have. At the time I had around $10 in my checking account. In fact, I didn't bring my checkbook with me because what would have been the point? I would never write a hot check. And, I was (duh) maxed out on my credit cards long before I ever accepted money from my family members.

Faster than a speeding train, one by one I began calling everyone I knew. As God would have it, each member of my family wasn't picking up the phone—either at work, OR at home, OR on their cell phones. For real.

One by one I called each of my friends, and the same thing happened with each of them. Until the very last (but not least) friend I had, did. Without hesitation, she gave me her credit card number to pay the entire balance, with one stipulation: that I never pay her back. Ever. Whether or not I liked it, I had no choice but to accept her offer; so, I did.

And drove home as fast as I could—without speeding. LOL

About six months later, her sweet mom had knee surgery, and she was concerned about taking off so much time from work. I quickly volunteered to pick her mom up and take her to physical therapy three times a week, and my friend quickly accepted. Companies were continuing to lay off people and she said she couldn't be taking off work several days a week for four to five hours per day. "Consider me paid in full," she said.

When God Moves—Checkmate!

These two years were so hard, but this layoff was such a blessing in disguise. I didn't realize it was the Holy Spirit in me at the time, giving me all these crazy ideas, but I know now, it was. Through daily prayer, meditation and reading my Bible, wisdom was being poured into me instead of doubt and fear.

This period of my life ushered in the first of many significant changes that would alter the landscape of my life forever. These changes would begin creating the woman I am becoming.

As a hardworking, exhausted, overworked and underpaid single mom, I was about as miserable as any human being could be. There were many days when the only way I knew I was alive, was because somehow, I continued to breathe in and out.

Have you ever read something—or heard someone say something—that lit a match within you? It happened to me, on an ordinary day, during a miserable time of my life. One sentence, from one article, from one magazine, changed the course of my life forever.

Although I don't recall the precise words it went something like this: 'If you don't like something in your life, change it. Do something. For if you continue to do nothing, what you've now is all you will ever have. You will never know who you were meant to be, or what you were capable of. Move. Speak Up. Write. Stop Whining and Do Something'. So, I did.

The perceived problem of making my career change a reality was that I didn't have a college degree. Back in those days, people told me I unless I had one, I would never—ever—be able to do jack-zip with my life. I'm in no way, shape or form devaluing education. I just hated sitting in a classroom all day trying to learn things that were of absolutely no interest to me. I still remember how shocked I was to learn I was actually able to graduate from high school. LOL

I believed what I was told for many years, just as I believe the husband I have today, loves me. That is, until that magazine article woke me up and got my attention.

"Have I not commanded you? Be strong and courageous! Do not tremble or be dismayed, for the Lord your God is with you wherever you go."
—Joshua 1:7

I contacted an editor from a newspaper for one of America's top 10 largest metropolitan cities, introduced myself, pitched a story idea and asked, "Please, will you not give me a chance by letting me write this for you? If you don't like it, you will not be under any obligation to print it. I just want someone who knows what they are doing, to read my writing and tell me if I have an ounce of talent. I will respect your decision, come what may, and you will never hear from me again."

As any good editor would, she asked for my credentials, to which I had none. It was beyond embarrassing to say "no", but I did it anyway. Sometimes it pays to be embarrassed, and this was one of them. I reminded her that I was happy to do the work, turn it in, and if I never heard from her again, at least I would know my dream wasn't meant to be.

The first of many miracles in my life, I owe to her, because she said, "Sure."

Running on instincts I didn't know I had, flying by the seat of my pants, I interviewed sources for the article, wrote and then submitted it to her. No one was more surprised than me when I heard back from her. She planned to run the article, and needed my address to send a check for my work. "Would you like another writing assignment for the paper?"

You know that feeling when your heart suddenly drops out of your body and into the earth at warp speed? That was me, in that unforgettable moment.

And thus began an almost 15-year freelance writing career with the newspaper.

During this time I also began reaching out to various local magazines and smaller publications, slowly building my resume as a writer/editor. It was exhilarating and although I didn't earn much, it was a much-needed boost to my low self-esteem. I also worked as a contract employee for an employment agency, every chance I got.

About one year after I was laid off, I began thinking about contacting local energy publications, and did. All of them said they used staff only (no freelancers), but one of the editors I spoke to was so kind and such a good conversationalist. We ended up chatting for close to two hours, and before getting off the phone he asked me to send some clippings of articles I'd written, out of personal interest only. He wasn't the publisher, had no hiring authority, so I had no reason to get my hopes up and I also had no reason not to honor his request. So, I did.

Samantha continued to grow, and I felt so bad that I couldn't afford to give her what I thought she needed to have. We shopped at Goodwill and other resale stores, clipped coupons and whatever else I could think of to save money.

The Time I Lost My Mind

Throughout my layoff I worked now and then as a contract temporary employee through various employment agencies. And, man, it just seemed like I would NEVER get a freaking break. I just hated, hated, hated, accepting handouts from my sister Elizabeth and Henry, but when you're a single parent, you do what have to do. Something was always going wrong. And the thing about it was, I couldn't for the life of me understand why I felt God was preventing me from asking them for more help to put out the "fire of the day". I have never heard His audible voice, but I know when He tells me stuff.

Samantha and I happened to be living in the cheapest apartment I could find when I was laid off. It was always important to me that she have as much stability in her life as possible, which meant keeping her in the same school district and attending classes with her same friends. The "apartment" was actually considered a "townhouse" and was managed by a property management company that, well, let me just say they didn't manage, well.

It was a hot July morning, made even hotter because our air conditioner had gone out for like at least the fifth time in about as many weeks. For real. The property manager was irate that I was on the phone explaining the situation, and said she would begin charging me $75 for each repair.

Although I can't remember the conclusion of this particular phone call, I will never forget what happened next.

When Samantha was dropped off by her friend's mom after a slumber party the night before, I had a small bag packed for each of us and told her I had a surprise.

I took us to what I lovingly refer to as 'Hotel Joe'. As soon as we opened the door to our rinky-dink-stink hotel room and threw our bags on the floor, we playfully danced around because for the first time in a long time, we had AIR CONDITIONING. Air conditioning that actually worked. #itsnottheheatitsthehumidity

After we both showered and were in our pajamas, I'm not too prideful to admit that—yes—we actually jumped up and down on the bed with such happiness and gratitude, that we had AIR CONDITIONING. If you've never been to the South in the summertime and tried to exist in a building without air conditioning that works, you can't know how much we appreciated this luxury. Needless it to say, we slept like children without a care in the world.

The next morning I took us to BREAKFAST at Hotel Joe. I wanted—needed—to pretend like we were on vacation. And that I was a good mother. A good mother who was a Normal Person. A Person with a Job. It made my heart sing, watching my daughter enjoy her chocolate chip pancakes, just like my beloved Aunt Jane used to make when I was little.

After we checked out, I took Samantha to another friend's house to spend the day. Why hang out in a hot apartment with an unemployed mom when you can have fun with your girlfriend?

Here's the point in this true story where I believe I lost my mind temporarily.

I didn't drive back to the apartment right away. Filled with an intense anger over my situation, I was also (surprisingly) faced with an equally ridiculous challenge from God to trust Him yet again, without knowing what the future would hold for me.

I sensed very strongly from Him that it was time to move and upgrade our living conditions, in spite of not having a full-time job. I visited several apartment complexes in the area and after falling in love with one in particular, I plopped down around a $300 required deposit for a (freaking) brand new apartment, one that had never been lived in.

Without a full-time job.

Oh, I had a job, alright, working as an administrative assistant. It was a long-term contract assignment and I was incredibly grateful because I didn't have to accept help from my family during this time. But the thing is, that contract could have ended the following Monday, for all I knew. Hek.

But on that day, I had had it. I didn't care if I lived. I didn't care if I died. And I even didn't care if I lost the temp job and they evicted us the next day. To no longer care, is a scary, dark place to be. I wanted ONE day, and ONE night, in an apartment with my daughter—an apartment with air-conditioning.

Now, I'm obviously not suggesting that anyone who is laid off go out and intentionally increase their rent by $300 per month, without a full-time job. This was God's path for me at this point in my life.

But this is what I did, because I had either lost my mind, or I was obeying what I believed with all my heart, God was challenging me to do.

It's called "walking by faith and not by sight." And walk, I did, right into an incredible, unbelievable, future I had yet to discover.

Less than a month later I saw an ad in the paper for an editorial position for a local publishing company. For those who aren't in the journalism/press media industry, editorial positions are few and far between. In fact, I can honestly say this was the first one I'd ever seen advertised since I was laid off.

I created two resumes: one for administrative positions and one for a writing type position. For the latter, I was able to include the many publications my work was featured in, along with the editorial award I received.

I was beyond excited when I sent the resume, but at the same time, highly doubtful I would hear from anyone, because I didn't have a college degree. Being raped by a fellow student without justice or the courage to seek counseling will do that to a girl. I was so messed up by that experience that my feet just couldn't walk towards ANY college campus.

But that's A-OK, because guess what?

My phone rang a few days later and the publisher of the company was on the other line, asking for an interview, which occurred a few days later. I was as nervous as a cat on a hot tin roof, but did my best. The following week I was called back for a second interview, this time in a conference room surrounded by several editors and art directors—colleagues who the new employee would be working with. I felt like I was testifying before Congress, I was so nervous!

Suddenly and without warning, one of the lead editors of the company's top publication realized it was me he spoke with on the phone a year earlier, for over an hour. I couldn't make this stuff up if I tried.

I get that this isn't going to make sense to anyone, but when I received a job offer the following day for the position, I can't tell you how scared I was. The enemy of my soul kept screaming in my ear, 'Who do you think you are? You don't have a college degree. You can't possibly do this. If you take this job you'll lose it within days, and THEN where will you be?'

Here's how frightened I was: when one of the men I worked for through the contract job walked by my cubicle and saw me in a puddle of tears, he sat down and asked what was wrong. I explained my dilemma and he was just the nicest man, listening to me at a time when no one ever seemed to do so.

He asked me to come into his office in five minutes, and when I did so there were several other fellow colleagues in there, all offering me such support and encouragement. I will never, ever forget their words: "It will be the biggest mistake of your life if you don't accept this position. We've seen what you're capable of, and we know you can do this. We KNOW it.

"Jobs like what you're doing are a dime a dozen, and from what we've heard, you've earned your stripes and proven yourself. It takes tremendous courage to just call someone at the newspaper and ask to submit an article when you've never written one in your life. If you didn't have the ability to write, she would have NEVER published your work, paid you for it and continue to send assignments to you all this time. You need to do this."

The irony didn't escape me, that when the HR manager of this company learned I had been offered a full-time position with benefits, suddenly I was presented with a job offer with their firm. A very good job offer. Isn't it just like Satan to tempt me while at the same time, tormenting me with doubt, fear and unbelief?

Thank God and ONLY God, I jumped in mid-air off the proverbial cliff and accepted the position. Just as when I first started writing for my city's top newspaper without a clue as to what I was doing—I did the job anyway, running on the instincts and love of everything about the business. As I began traveling around the country, meeting new people, asking questions, learning new things and then getting to write about it, I just couldn't *believe* I was getting paid for my efforts. The career change of my dreams. No kidding!

I can do all things through Him Who strengthens me.—Philippians 4:13

Ouch, God, But Thank-You

Within months of accepting the job, I was asked to write a cover story for the company's leading magazine. This kind of opportunity just doesn't happen to someone like me, but here's the thing. It did. I covered a milestone anniversary of one of the world's largest pipelines, and had an absolute blast doing so. Although I would eventually begin writing about other areas of the energy industry, my first love was always pipelines. I was fascinated by them.

One year an industry association's group somewhere in New Jersey invited me to attend their equipment operator training compound in hopes I would consider it worthy of covering in a future issue.

I had the BEST TIME! While I don't recall all the details about the training camp, I remember it being many acres and having all types of construction and equipment to be used by the trainees. There were numerous areas of intentionally created terrain, including trenches of different depths, railroad track, hills, man-made creeks, etc. Attendees had to master each piece of equipment in all different terrains before graduating and being sent off to various pipeline projects around the world.

"Old Fart Frank" (as I fondly remember him) was such a hoot. When he asked if I wanted to climb aboard a pipeline sideboom machine, naturally I took him up for it like any good reporter. (Google 'pipeline sideboom' to see how big these can be). They yelled instructions from the ground, and sure enough I was able to move the long arm carrying the pipe towards the trench, when suddenly the whole dang machine began falling over on its side.

Never had I ever been a damsel in distress like this! What woman wouldn't love seeing tons of men running towards her to save her? LOL

All ended up just fine, and Old Fart Frank decided in his infinite wisdom, to make me an offer to either go to the Jersey Shore or a quick 4-hour tour of New York City. I couldn't pass up going to the Big Apple, especially with a personal tour guide. We had so much fun. Sorry for the sidetrack, I couldn't resist that fun memory!

Back to my cover story for one of the energy industry's leading magazines. Upon publication, I received a personal invitation from the company president to attend the company's festivities in Alaska. Alaska! Me! I was beyond excited and so honored. Unfortunately it didn't last long. I became filled with rage when the publisher chose another editor to attend in my place. I WAS THE ONE WHO WORKED SO HARD AND WROTE THE STORY! In hindsight, <u>of course</u> the publisher was right in choosing the lead editor of this magazine over a young pup like me. Who in the world did I think I was? LOL

The next morning I began looking for another job and accepted a managing editor position in the telecommunications industry the following month. My publisher came and asked why I was leaving, i.e. did I want more money, and my pride just blew up like my waistline after the holidays. I told him no, that I just wanted a job offering more responsibility.

Chapter 4

Brighter Days

The new job with more responsibility and a high-pollutin' job title brought me incredible misery. Truly, it was the disciplining hand of God for being so full of pride. Believe it or not, I rarely drank through this period.

During the brief time I worked for this company, an editor from another significantly larger international energy publishing company began pursuing me to come work for him. To this day I have no idea how he found me, as back then I don't think Google existed. I was very flattered but also terrified to make a move. After all, look where my bright idea to switch jobs, got me. LOL

God, with such infinite mercy and grace, intervened. Within three months of accepting the job I held at the time, the company announced it was relocating to Chicago. If I wanted to keep my job, I had to relocate.

My daughter was always my priority, and there was no way I was yanking her out of school with the friends she had grown up with since kindergarten. The same day I received this news, the guy from the editor from the large energy publishing house called. We met that afternoon after work for an interview. By the end of the week I accepted an incredible job offer.

Only God can switch things up like this in my life. Not only that, but only God could help me write coherent articles about energy technologies <u>to this day</u>, I *still* don't understand! I was where He wanted me to be at the time, in His perfect will for my life, and without His help, I would have been toast, that's all there is to it.

Unlike my first editorial job, this one required international travel. In a beautiful unexpected moment of poetic justice, when filling out my passport application I had to include the birthplace of both ex-husbands. Contacting my second ex- filled me with such anxiety, so I phoned his mother, who I loved dearly and hated saying goodbye to because of the divorce.

I explained I was working as the managing editor for a local magazine and preparing to attend the annual conference overseas. The passport's requirements stated that I needed her son's place of birth, among other items of information, for approval, and this was the purpose of my call.

I have to admit, it was fun thinking about my second ex-husband's reaction to this news. The 'little woman' he made fun of and talked down to years ago had found a way to make her dreams come true.

If possible, so far as it depends on you, be at peace with all men. Never take your own revenge, beloved, but leave room for the wrath of God, for it is written, "VENGEANCE IS MINE, I WILL REPAY," says the Lord.—Romans 12:18-19

Believe it or not, several years later during a downturn in the economy, I was laid off for a second time, still a single mom. My reaction to my boss must have blown his mind: "Oh, that's OK,

Bill. It just means God has something better for me to do." No tears, no fears.

Three weeks later I fell 16 feet out of the tree in my backyard. With no job, no spare money and no boyfriend, I was trying to prune it myself and lost my balance off the ladder. When you're falling 16 feet, believe me, you've got time to consider what's happening, how much it's going to hurt, and what's the best way to land. Charlie's Angels' style: on all fours, in case you ever find yourself in a similar position.

So there I was, alone in my backyard. It's nothing but a miracle that I didn't break my neck, back, or hip. I knew I injured myself because of the pain, but stubborn lass that I am, I got up and was startled to realize I could barely walk. I hobbled into the house and called my best friend, who lived 10 minutes away. She took me to the ER, where I learned I had a broken leg, messed up knee and elbow.

A week later I'm in my home office, howling at the moon in pain. "God, are you KIDDING ME? WHY have You allowed me to lose my job again, and WHY this accident? Uhm, Hell-O? I'm howling at the moon in pain and can't walk without a cane. Oh, and yeah, I need a new job."

Lickety-split, He answered my question, although no, not audibly. Apparently He wanted me to write a book. LOL. We had a verbal ping pong conversation back and forth, where I told Him He had the wrong person, I'm not a pastor, Bible study teacher or anything else. I'm just one of 500-trillion humans He's created since the world was brought forth into existence—nothing more, nothing less. And that I have never written a book before, and I'm not smart enough, spiritual enough, 'anything' enough. "Exactly," He spoke to my spirit. Gulp.

This conversation went on for about three weeks, until I knew He wasn't going to quit riding my back like no tomorrow. I sat in my home office, right leg propped up on the trash can for any kind of relief, put my fingers on the keyboard, and said, "OK". And so it went.

Loved ones, I'm not lying when I say my first book fell onto the screen. It was almost like an out of body experience.

In a matter of months, the book was finished, and I had no idea how to find a publisher. I went to Barnes & Noble and found an annual *Writer's Market*, a huge compilation of publishers of all types of periodicals, magazines and books worldwide, and sent query letters to as many as I could find who might be interested. All of this cost money I needed to pay the mortgage, car loan, etc. This book was God's idea and I knew He would take care of Samantha and I, just as He had done so beautifully during my first two-year layoff, years earlier. I was starting to get angry.

And we know God causes all things to work together for good to those who love Him, to those who are called according to His good purpose.
—Romans 8:28

Rejection letters poured in, but sometimes there would be handwritten notes of encouragement, saying the book was great and much-needed in the world, it just didn't fit under the umbrella of publishing their company was known for. One day I somehow found a website called Writers Edge Service, where publishers troll looking for books to buy. In order for a prospective author's manuscript to be accepted and published on this site, one has to submit a book proposal and three sample chapters. The editors at Writers Edge Service review the material, and if they believe it has merit, it gets posted on the site for publishers to find—for a period of five years.

My work was accepted, and while I was stoked, I still needed a job. I was angry at God because my knee still hurt, and I was doing everything I could to find work. "God, this was YOUR idea, not mine. I have been obedient, I have done all I can to find a publisher. This is YOUR problem. If You want it published, You've to bring the publisher. I'm outta here because hell-O? I NEED A JOB!" I still can't believe I talked to Him that way.

Sacrificial Obedience, God's Response

At some point during my second layoff, through a prayer request shared by a member of my Bible study class, I learned about a single mom of three kids who suffered from MS, in need of transportation to the medical center for appointments on a regular basis.

There's no question in my mind that Deanna was my "homework" during this period of my life. I reached out and offered to be her driver, as long as she understood I needed to do what I could to look for work each day before heading over to her apartment.

We bonded quickly and deeply, supporting each other through our respective—albeit different forms of—pain. Never in my life had I ever seen any human being suffer so much, as Deanna. Her husband left her a week after her diagnosis, she lost custody of her kids because she was unable to take care of them, and pretty much anything that could break in a person's life, was broken, in hers.

As you may or may not imagine, due to the severity of her dire circumstances and intense, almost always ongoing physical pain, Deanna was one of the strongest Christians I ever knew. There were days she was in so much pain, I would just lie on the bed next to her, and together, we cried.

When she became too cold, I would put a sheet over her and then she would scream from the pain, so then she would become too cold again. Repeat. Once Christmas she was suicidal, and I was terrified—feeling very responsible for keeping her alive. You can imagine I talked to God a lot about this. Anyway—I am extremely grateful to call her one of my closest friends. She's doing so much better these days, thanks to an experimental trial she's participating in.

Shortly after receiving my income tax refund, with part of the money I allowed myself to buy a much-needed new computer to help with my job search, among other things.

As I began to unpack the box, I remembered what an absolute clunker piece of junk, Deanna's computer was. If you're old enough to remember computer monitors being about two feet thick and floppy discs to insert in the hard drives, you will quickly get the picture.

Although it hurt me to do this, I decided to keep the new computer in its wrapping and give it to her, because God knows, she needed it far more than I. Her electronic dinosaur was incredibly slow, and because of her health and overall situation, if she was not fighting with the Social Security office about disability checks, she was plowing through the nightmare of trying to reach someone handling her Medicaid.

Deanna burst into tears when I gave her the new computer. The joy and gratitude she expressed that day were worth the sacrifice. It is so, so much better to give, than receive.

When I left her apartment, I went to a local ministry to try and get help with some of my expenses, because my car was on its last leg and in need of expensive car repairs that I was unable to afford. Keep in mind that God specifically made it clear that I was NOT to ask Henry or Elizabeth for any more money than they were already giving me each month.

I needed to decide whether to pay the mortgage and utilities, or get the car fixed so I could make it to any job interviews I might have and escort Deanna to her doctor appointments. Oh. And also buy food, gas and prescription medications my daughter and I needed. Minor stuff like that.

"You have too much income," the lady replied, after reviewing the massive paperwork I was required to complete. I seriously couldn't believe my ears, but it's true. That's exactly what she said. Where all of this income was, I didn't know, because the minute the checks I received from Henry and Elizabeth came in, it was gone as quickly as it took for me to write the checks that would 'keep the lights on', if you get what I am saying. My unemployment benefits were long gone, by this time.

I drove home in tears, hoping Samantha wasn't there. Thankfully she wasn't. When I checked the mail before going into the house, I stopped in the driveway and opened a hand-addressed envelope.

As God is my witness, here is what was inside: a check for $1,500 from a couple I didn't know and had never heard of, for that matter. There was also a note with one of the kindest things anyone has ever said (in this case, written) to me.

"Dear Paulette,

We were so moved by your advocating for help on Deanna's behalf when you shared her story after Bible study last Sunday. There you were, standing with crutches and also a single mother and out of work—not asking for help for yourself, but for someone else. We thought you could use a little help, yourself. This is a gift, and we do not wish to be repaid."

The estimate for my car repairs was around $1,400, which left me with enough money to buy groceries and gas for the next several weeks.

Once again I want to reinforce that God works through others, sometimes as in this case, the kindness of strangers, to answer our prayers. Although I didn't make what was to me at the time a hard sacrifice by giving Deanna that new computer expecting to receive anything in return, God came through for me in spades that day.

I wrote down the name and address of the couple who so generously made my day when I had just experienced such a cruel rejection for help, before cashing the check. Imagine, if you will, how happy I was to send them a thank-you note many months later, to let them know I had finally received a good job offer and how good, God is.

One of my other favorite examples of how God answers prayer, is the time I thought it was a swell idea to try and teach a Bible study class during the week at my church. If you only knew me, you would know how funny this is. Suffice it to say, I was not called to teach. Like, anything. Ever. But I like to try new things, there was a need at the church, and I gave it a go. Nothing ventured, nothing gained! Nevertheless, there I was one night with a table full of students of all ages.

At the end of the class, it is common for teachers to ask if there are any prayer requests, write them down and then lead everyone in praying for others. After taking notes from everyone, I shared my own prayer request regarding Deanna's situation before praying for them all.

The following day I received an email from one of the attendees. Although I don't recall her name, she explained her husband had left her "well off". She went on to say she was moved by Deanna's dire, painful life, and wanted to help. By offering to pay her 3-bedroom, 2-bath apartment's rent. For an entire year. And with one stipulation: that Deanna never know her (the widow's) name or contact information.

I quickly accepted her offer, and arranged for this to happen with the apartment manager, who (like me) was positively stunned. Once again I was so happy to share this news with Deanna, and we cried in joyful gratitude to God for His incredible goodness, once again.

What is interesting to me, is how God worked in this situation, because although I can't remember exactly what happened next, other than to say this was the only class I ever taught. Teaching—for sure—is not my gift. LOL

Speaking of friends, I would be remiss not to mention my other friends—Dina, Suzanne, Carla and Cathy—who I couldn't have made it through these layoffs (and life), without. Diana helped me on an entertainment level by taking us out for long drives in her convertible Mustang, listening to music and an occasional rom-com movie.

Suzanne paid my utility bills in exchange for me taking her elderly mom to and from physical therapy appointments for several months, thus preventing her from having to take off work and risk being laid off for missing work. Carla and I also bartered for services.

As a hairdresser, she styled my hair before job interviews in exchange for me babysitting her newborn son. Cathy surprised me with a large check for no reason other than she could afford to do so at the time.

Henry and Elizabeth continued to supplement my monthly income to help me meet my monthly expenses, but there were so many instances where needs arose and God specifically forbid me from asking them for money. He wanted to prove to me that He and only He, was my Source for everything.

About 10 months passed, and it was getting to the point where I couldn't walk, even with a cane or walker. My broken leg had healed, but the knee was only getting worse. Desperate times call for desperate measures. I made a proposition to my orthopedic doctor, that being if I were able to write an article for the newspaper about his practice, would he agree to look at and treat my knee? "Why yes!" he said.

When it was discovered I had a torn meniscus and needed knee surgery, he arranged for a fellow surgeon to do the procedure, made sure the hospital charged 50% of its normal day rate for outpatient surgery and create a payment plan I could afford. #Miracle

Time marched on, I continued to help Deanna and God continued to provide for Samantha and I through my siblings and freelance writing opportunities. We lived check-to-check, like always, after having stripped the family budget to bare bones. It wasn't fun, but I learned so much during my first layoff, that we never felt like we were missing anything.

My beloved mother, who I made peace with years earlier, had remarried and relocated to Montana. She came into town for Mother's Day and enjoyed spending time with each of her children and their families. Mother decided to visit her cardiologist for a check-up, since doctors in the medical center were so highly esteemed, and were more experienced than those in the small community where she lived.

Much to our surprise, she had a huge blockage and emergency surgery was performed the following day. She came through it just fine, and was put on the eighth floor for a week of observation before returning home to Montana. We all agreed this was a good idea, because of her age and history with heart problems.

So painful to remember, I will share only the most pertinent details. Mistakes were made, she ended up in a coma in ICU for 10 days before her organs shut down and she passed away. We never knew if she could hear us praying over her, talking and singing to her, or if she could even feel our hugs and holding of hands. I remember driving to the hospital using my crutch on the gas pedal, in so much pain.

The night she passed away, I remember talking to God and saying, "God, this REALLY hurts. WHERE IS YOUR ANSWER TO ROMANS 8:28 IN THIS SITUATION?"

Of all the many promises of God found in the Bible, this is the one He has fulfilled in my life, the most. Some things in my life I'll never forget, and this was one of them. At precisely 1:30 am I woke up with an idea to being start an unofficial ministry sitting with elderly seniors while they were hospitalized.

The following day, using money I couldn't really afford to use on something so frivolous, I ordered a magnetic car sign for $60 that had these words and my cell phone number on it as a cheap way to advertise what God had put on my heart. I didn't want ANYONE to go through what my beloved mother went through, or my precious siblings and I went through, watching her slip away. We trusted the doctors and nurses to take care of her, and look what happened in spite of it all.

What's ironic, is I received many calls but only from people who wanted to work for me. I thanked them for calling, but explained that especially in light of what happened to my mom, I only trusted myself with such an important job. God, in His infinite wisdom, always brought the people He wanted me to look after, in ways only He can do (similar to the unexpected friendship with Deanna, a total stranger at the time).

My lay (unofficial) ministry was a way for me to earn much-need income on an occasional basis, and it was extremely rewarding. I never offered actual healthcare services of any type or administered medication. My role was to be present with the elderly parent when their adult children were unable to do so. I kept daily journals by the hour, so the siblings and/or spouse of the elderly person knew precisely what happened. Giving someone peace of mind is an incredibly rewarding thing to do.

A few months went by, and suddenly I noticed an ad for a regional editor for a healthcare magazine. When I read the job description, I thought surely it was too good to be true. While it's true I'd been wanting a job all this time, I really, really wanted THIS job, and applied for it as quickly as I could.

During the second phone interview (since the company was out of state), the editor explained she mailed a copy of the magazine to each job candidate. Our assignment was to read it and suggest three new story ideas based on something we read from the content. After reviewing the entries, a third and final interview would be conducted in-person.

I had zero problems falling to my knees and praying, "God, I want THIS job. No other job. THIS job. Please show me what I can do to pole vault over everyone else and get THIS job."

After reviewing the magazine and developing the requested three potential story ideas, I had another insane idea, that being to contact the head of a special task force in the medical center whose purpose was to develop and annually practice a strategic plan among all hospitals in the event of a pandemic or other citywide emergency. As a side note, never did I ever think at the time, a pandemic such as Co-Vid would infect the planet years later in 2020.

I contacted the leading physician in charge of the task force (which included members of all hospital chains in the medical center). After introducing myself by my name only, I explained my interest in the task force because I was working on an article about it, and asked if he were available for an interview. The following week I met with him, and barely even understanding what a pandemic was, by the grace of God alone, I posed what he said were thoughtful and intelligent questions, and was pleased to answer them.

Now stop for a second, and understand why this is another miracle. In the media, it is always necessary to have a job title with a publishing company or news outlet to secure an interview with anyone. At the very least, if you're a freelance writer, you must provide the name of the publication in which the article will appear.

I had neither, because I was laid off and the editor of the magazine I was interviewing with, had no clue what I was up to. The article was written and emailed the following day.

But He said, "The things that are impossible with people are possible with God."
—Luke 18:27

A week later, when I walked into the hotel lobby to meet the editor in person, she had a copy of the article in her hand, beaming, asking, "How did you DO this?!" Apparently not only did she love the submission, she pulled the original cover story for the next month's issue and placed mine in the top stop, instead. In the field of journalism, trust me, this just DOESN'T happen. #butGod…

I flew up to corporate headquarters the following week for in-person training, and I was finally—finally—working again. You can't know how much fun I had with this job. God used this job to heal my broken heart over the needless, sudden death of my mom as a result of gross medical negligence.

For the most part, I was responsible for generating story ideas, deciding who and where to go within my region to interview, which press conferences to attend, then obviously doing the work and submitting the articles on time.

The editor held weekly meetings with the editorial team to discuss each month's issue, determine progress rates, etc. I discovered a gift I didn't know I had, that being to generate unique and compelling story ideas. I was like a machine; I couldn't stop. She was elated, of course, so much so that she said she'd created a separate email folder entitled "Paulette's ideas". LOL

Day and night, night and day, I was constantly emailing her with potential story ideas. I lived, breathed and exhaled this job, 24/7. It was so easy to walk down the short hallway to my home office at all hours of the night, doing so. And thus, my year's long nightmare a/k/a chronic insomnia was born.

About a year into the job, I received an unexpected phone call from one of the most highly revered elderly pastors of my beloved church. I recognized his voice immediately, and was befuddled as to how he got my number, and the purpose of his call. I kept wondering if I was in trouble, and if so, why? LOL

Apparently he heard about the now defunct ministry through other pastors and people of our church, and asked if I would please consider helping him take care of Betty, his wife of 66 years, who was recently diagnosed with Alzheimer's, a disease I knew little about.

Because I recognized the seriousness of the situation, I didn't take this request lightly and didn't hurry to make a decision. I strive to be someone who keeps their word, and I didn't want to let him down a week or two later. I met with this beautiful couple several times in their home over the course of a month, before agreeing to come there and care for her three days during the week and on Sunday mornings. I packed up the company laptop and necessary materials and while she slept during the day, I worked on my articles.

Life became incredibly, incredibly stressful. Alzheimer's is a beast I wouldn't ever take on again unless it was a family member or friend. The magazine—initially a monthly when I started work—suddenly became bi-monthly. I was expected to deliver twice the content and twice the travel, for the same amount of pay. My heart was with the pastor and his family, but the publishing job was what paid the bills. My insomnia never stopped, and only got worse.

Thankfully one morning the pastor explained the senior pastor of the church asked him to propose to me that I quit the publishing job and work for him full-time. They offered to put me on staff at church payroll and pay me whatever I needed to support Samantha and I. To say I immediately burst into tears with relief is not only an understatement; it's the truth.

I don't think I have ever typed so quickly in all my life, as I zapped off a brief notice of resignation to my editor. The pastor, his wife and I had a huge group hug, although (of course) she was clueless as to why. She passed away about four years later, and he was reunited with his bride within the next several years.

During this time, I also took on a part-time weekend job as manager of a self-storage facility because I was determined to become debt-free. I never wanted to owe anyone anything again as long as I lived. All of this to say, for one and one-half years I held down one full-time job and two part-time jobs, none of which helped my insomnia. I couldn't sleep, so I figured I might as well work.

Chapter 5

Third Time's a Charm

Within a few months of my new full-time caregiver role, someone paid for a free three- (or six?) month membership to Match.com. I guess they either didn't believe I was 10-million percent content with my life as a divorced single mom; or, they wanted me to find someone to spend the rest of my life with (for real, this time).

Guilt over not being interested practically strangled me to death, so I created a stupid profile and endured the process. The first two dates with two different men were fine. They were each intelligent professionals, one an ER physician and the other, a dentist. Very nice, zero chemistry.

I'm a girl who needs chemistry.

Right before closing out of my account one day, the photo of one man's face caught my eye, and I did something extraordinary (for me): I sent him a message. I truly think it was a God-situation, because I have never been someone who chases after men, not after all the trouble they've given me. LOL

He responded back and said I was on his radar, but he was presently communicating with another woman and wanted to see where it led. "I'm not someone who plays the field," and I found that so impressive and it was my first clue that he was a man of truth and integrity.

The following week I heard back from him, and he said the woman was a former doctor's wife and he sensed she was looking for a new husband who would provide her with the same benefits, and he wasn't interested in her type.

We chatted online back and forth for about a month, before graduating to phone calls. After three months we agreed to meet in person for coffee. Well, the chemistry lab was up and running, because that coffee became an all-day first date that ended with dinner later that night.

We literally couldn't take our eyes off each other, or stop talking. I specifically remember when finally saying goodnight, walking to my car.

I turned around to look at him once more, and found him standing in place, looking at me. Simultaneous waves; simultaneous smiles.

By the third date I told him 'how the cow ate the cabbage' (as we say in the South). I explained that I'm not your normal woman (huge understatement-LOL). After two failed marriages and a gazillion horrible dates and relationships, I'd come to realize that doing things the world's way never worked for me. I explained to him that before I agreed with myself to create a profile on Match, I vowed to God I would follow His ways of getting to know someone of the opposite sex.

<u>Translation</u>: I flat out told him that no matter how nice he treated me, no matter what he bought me, no matter where he took me, NO MATTER WHAT, I would never give away parts of myself to a man outside of marriage again. "I wholeheartedly understand if you want to part ways at this time, I also understand how archaic this must sound. But you need to understand, that you will never be first place in my life."

Before I proceed, please know that I don't share this personal information to judge or condemn anyone. I take Matthew 7:1 very seriously! LOL

You could've knocked me over with a feather, when he immediately agreed to my terms, saying his mom was a devout Christian and he was raised as such.

With me being a journalist and he being in a profession requiring extreme analytical skills, I suggested that we get to know each other better by using a book I found with a title of something like 'things to ask before you get married'. Our dates—whether they be coffee, lunch, dinner, attending church and walks in the park after—always included what can only be referred to as Q&A time.

I know how this must sound, but it was actually very fun and served a higher purpose. If you just think about it, how else are you really going to get to know someone, if you don't ask questions and they don't answer? We agreed on three questions per date, and every time I asked him something and he answered, I always followed back with my answer. Fair's fair.

Of the many things that impressed me about Preston, was his continued honesty and integrity. The writer in me recognized the author of this Q&A book's clever tactics. I began to realize throughout the book, the same very important questions were being asked now and then, only using different language. Preston's answer remained the same, each and every time. My self-esteem increased and I could look myself in the mirror again.

I guess as time went on and I didn't stray from my personal boundaries, in his eyes I became a woman worth marrying. Men always value that which they perceive they can't have. He later admitted the 'caveman hunter' instinct must've come out in him, because he was determined to win my hand as well as my heart.

We thoroughly enjoyed an ole-timey' courtship for one and one-half years, before he proposed. I said "OK, but not until I'm out of debt." It was deeply personal and important to me that I enter this marriage without debt, so I waited. I think it meant a lot to Preston to know I was marrying him for love, and not money. Money alone is just nothing, and not worth my life, that's for sure. LOL. The pastor I worked for provided wise pre-marital counseling for us in his home. To top it all off, he married us in the same small chapel where my mom's memorial service was held.

Do you see how beautifully God tied up so many loose ends and healed my broken heart in so many ways? The pastor was like a father to me, and the peace I had every morning at their breakfast table, him sharing devotions and praying for Samantha and I, was something I never took for granted. I was in an extremely privileged position, as I knew numerous pastors and staff members would have given anything to have 24/7 direct access to his love, wisdom and prayers and support.

Afterwards we had a huge dinner reception at a nearby Italian restaurant, and we were so surprised by the number of people who said it was the best, most meaningful wedding they'd ever attended. And, I agree. Given our mutual faithfulness to God, I have zero shame in telling you what a great wedding night we had. Talk about passion, romance and sizzle! #worththewait

As a side note, Preston and I just celebrated our 15th honeymoon earlier this year. We still flirt shamelessly like teenagers in love, and just have the *best time ever*. I believe when we honor God, especially going against the insane society we live in, our radical obedience brings an abundance of blessings and joy this world will never know, much less provide. We laugh all the time about how neither of us knew marriage could actually be FUN, and get better instead of worse, over time. #besthusbandEVER!

So, remember the book I wrote almost five years earlier? Four years and 51 weeks ago, to be precise? With less than a week to go before the five-year term of my sample chapters and book proposal were to be removed from that publisher/author website, out of the clear blue sky I remembered it and that I needed to change my name and contact information to reflect my new married name, email, home address, etc.

Do you honestly think this was my own brilliant mind that just *happened* to remember all of this just in the knick of time? Please. We both know it wasn't me. LOL

A few days later while Preston was in Italy at a business conference, I received an email from a publishing company wanting a copy of my manuscript.

My WHAT?!

I remember writing back and saying I hoped I could find it, due to the recent marriage, relocation to a new home, and I still had boxes in my closet to unpack. This was so long ago, anyone who remembers tiny floppy discs will understand what I'm saying. LOL

Lo and behold and to make a long story short, they offered me a traditional publishing contract for the book. This rarely, rarely, rarely happens for an unknown author.

"I know that You can do all things, And that no purpose of Yours can be thwarted."—Job 42:2

When Preston called one evening to check in on me, I asked him if he remembered me telling him I'd written a book a long time ago. You can't know how much fun it was to tell him I received a "real" publishing contract. Neither of us knew what to think, and I followed his advice to have an attorney look over the contract.

The book was released quite quickly, and although I was so grateful for the contract, I didn't like that they changed my title and I didn't like the cover. I started my own independent publishing company and wrote two additional books for people who are facing adversity, thus giving me full creative control. It was hard, learning how to do this, but also incredibly fun.

Years later the publisher of my first book was bought out by a large international publishing house. Before the sale closed, I asked them if they would please consider returning to me all first rights, to which they agreed.

This was important because having them meant I could re-publish it with the cover of my choosing; so, I did. Anyone who is a creative person understands how important it is to approve of the final product, and I was beyond grateful to God for making this a reality.

Chapter 6

In and Out of Alcohol Prison

Within three weeks after marrying and moving into Preston's home, I sold my little house located about an hour away. In many ways, the selling of that house is what really solidified in our hearts and minds that we were, indeed, husband and wife. It represented the happiest years of mine and Samantha's life at the time, and was a tremendous accomplishment for me as a single mom for so many years.

Unfortunately, I learned early on that Preston snores louder than I could ever sleep through. My insomnia was already so bad, and as a newlywed and woman who'd been sleeping without the safety and comfort of a loving, protective husband for almost 20 years, I desperately wanted nothing more than to share the same bed until death us do part, but this was not to be. I need to be able to sleep!

It wasn't long before exhaustion turned to anger and resentment, and we agreed on separate bedrooms because it was the only logical step. Preston refused to try wearing a CPAP machine, and having tried one myself years earlier before giving it away a week later, I didn't blame him. #nothappening!

One day I ran into an old friend at the mall, and it was as if no time had passed at all. She explained she was in town on business, and suggested we meet for dinner. We did so, and had the best time. During the course of the conversation I complained about my insomnia, and she suggested having a drink to help me relax and fall asleep.

It had never, not once, occurred to me in my entire life, to consider using alcohol for the drug that it is, to help cure my insomnia. When I say, 'using alcohol for the drug that it is', all my life until I began this journey to freedom from alcohol prison, did I ever know that alcohol is considered a drug by the National Institute of Drug Abuse (affiliated with the National Institute of Health) and the Mayo Clinic, among others.

The World Health Organization defines alcohol as "a toxic and psychoactive substance with dependence-producing properties". And that it's available over the counter (OTC) just blows my mind from here to eternity.

It's actually much worse than most OTC drugs, because it's been known for decades in the medical community to be a highly addictive carcinogenic toxic poison. But hey, let's not get ahead of ourselves because I didn't know these things at the time. I _definitely_ didn't know these things at the time.

I ran the idea by Preston when he got home, excited to give it a try. He agreed it was worth a shot, especially since drinking alcohol is considered ordinary behavior by everyone and neither of us thought it would possibly do any harm. After all, I used to drink off and on all my life without a problem. With the little bit of wine I drank that night, little did we know at the time, I had just checked myself into alcohol prison and the key to escaping it vanished in thin air.

Yes, _just like that_. I went from a social drinker to someone who initially became addicted to alcohol, seemingly overnight. In all actuality, it probably took hold within the first two weeks of this new practice. I say this with all honesty because I remember recognizing something in my mind/body had changed in a way I didn't understand.

In fact, I remember telling Preston that my brain itself had changed, but I couldn't explain how, or why. I just knew something was different.

Once you have that 'one drink', the one that ushers you into alcohol prison, it's too freaking late. You're in. The other thing you need to know, is that <u>no one knows</u> whether or not THEIR next drink will be the one that throws them in the pen. But if you're reading this book, chances are, you DO know these things.

Little did I know at the time, there actually was a scientific, physical explanation for the brain changes I noticed: neuroplasticity.

Wikipedia defines neuroplasticity as "the ability of neural networks in the brain to change through growth and reorganization. It is when the brain is rewired to function in some way that differs from how it previously functioned. These changes range from individual neuron pathways making new connections, to systemic adjustments like cortical remapping."

Wikipedia provides examples that include circuit and network changes resulting from learning a new ability, environmental influences, practice and psychological stress. "Neuroplasticity was once thought by neuroscientists to manifest only during childhood, but research in the latter half of the 20th century showed many aspects of the brain can be altered even through adulthood."

I was incredibly relieved to learn that I *wasn't* some crazy bad person because I developed an addiction to a highly promoted, legal, heavily-promoted addictive drug through repetitive use to help me fall asleep.

My brain initially recognized alcohol as a solution to my insomnia, and new neural pathways were formed through neuroplasticity. That's exactly how the addiction was formed, from a science-based perspective. From a spiritual perspective, I had allowed myself to get distracted by the people and things of this world instead of turning to God for help with the insomnia.

Every time I woke up in the middle of the night, I drank another glass of wine to fall back asleep. Alcohol WAS helping me fall asleep. It just wasn't helping me *stay* asleep. Unfortunately my girlfriend *couldn't* have BEEN <u>more wrong</u> in suggesting a drink to help me fall asleep. In fact, alcohol is the <u>very last thing</u> anyone should use, to help them fall asleep. Listen to the *Huberman Podcast*, Episode #86, "How Alcohol Affects Your Brain and Body" to learn why. Andrew Huberman, PhD is a neuroscientist who knows these things.

One glass became two, which morphed into a bottle of wine on some nights. After five or six years of this, sometimes (not always) I needed something stronger, so I turned to whiskey. 'What kind of good Christian woman does this?' I wondered. The kind whose brain had literally rewired itself to accommodate this new information, because that's what brains do.

I was drinking more than I ever had before, and it was happening several times a week. I had no control whatsoever, and it scared me. And if that weren't enough, I was struggling with guilt, shame and self-loathing because I couldn't stop drinking no matter how hard I tried.

Neuroplasticity in the brain creates a 'neural activity feedback loop'. That sounded exactly like how my brain was performing, because of my inability to control my alcohol intake once I started drinking it on nights when I hadn't slept in several days and I was desperate to sleep.

Society is SO GOOD about placing the blame on the individual, and not the physical components of the drug itself. And there are no warning labels about its addictive nature, and since it's so readily available, is it any wonder I hated myself for being unable to control that which I didn't understand?

HOW WAS IT that for many decades of drinking without *ever* having a problem with alcohol, that this would happen to me? And, why? Why now?

Anyone who knows me well, knows I'm anything but a timid mouse. When I decide to do something, I stop at nothing to get it done. The same holds true when there's something I want, as evidenced by my pursuing and achieving a writing career despite the odds.

How is it years earlier in my first editorial job, I was brave enough to be the only reporter at a press conference at a refinery to approach former Venezuelan President Hugo Chavez and score an exclusive story? Or teach myself how to self-publish, form my own independent publishing company, raise a fantastic adult woman without a spouse I could count on, survive sexual assault, harassment, two failed marriages, a challenging childhood or any other countless achievements, yet I was taken out by this inert liquid in a glass?

Wow—was I swimming in a cesspool of pride back then, or WHAT? But these were the questions I was asking myself at the time, never not once, being able to see the truth of the matter at hand.

Preston never knew of my addiction for a long time, because he was always at work and never saw it. I made sure I stopped in time to get my act together, look nice and have supper on the table when he walked in, so ready to love on him. I wanted to be the kind of wife he deserved.

Trying—and Failing—to Fit In

Having been laid off for the third and final time by the pastor whose wife I took care of, and with Preston at work all day, I was so lonely and—worst—bored out of my brains. Not a good combination, when you throw insomnia into the mix. People who value worldly things might say I had 'moved up in the world' by marrying Preston, and from that perspective they'd be right. But I'm not materialistic so I didn't care.

My new neighborhood was a far cry from the humble nest I had left behind. I was just a regular goldfish used to swimming in a fishbowl who suddenly found herself in an ocean full of beautiful female creatures and I definitely didn't fit in. Not only would Preston not understand how hard this was for me—NO man would be able to.

Women are wired for being social, men are wired to work and bring home the bacon. I felt like I had no purpose in life other than to keep a clean house and look nice, and while that's all well and good, it didn't take 10-12 hours a day to do so. I needed something more to fill my time, and there weren't that many hospital visits to be made through our church ministry on this new side of town I lived in.

I can't begin to tell you how difficult it was for me to try and make friends. And boy, did I ever try. For one thing, I visited many local churches and joined one for a short amount of time, before returning to the nearest location of the church home I have been a member of since 1999. This new location was 30-45 minutes away, so the friends I made there lived quite far away and none of us felt like driving that far on other days of the week to hang out together, myself included. I dearly loved Preston and being married to him, yet I also missed my girlfriends back home more than I realized.

I have found it's really hard for strangers to become friends unless they have an immediate common bond, and/or a regular excuse to get together, such as weekly Bible study or kids in school. Even then it can be difficult, because everyone seems to be so busy and off to do the next thing on their list after class. Perhaps that's just the way it is, and it depends on what season of life someone's in.

Me, I was retired and had all the time in the world. I was grateful to be in such a blessed position, but gosh was it ever hard getting used to. I was—and still am—so very much in love with Preston, but at the time he was still working. When he got home, we'd have supper, do the dishes and I'd be in bed by 8 pm because that's what my trio of healthcare professionals prescribed. My bedtime routine remains the same, years later, and we are more in love than ever, 15 years in! #praiseGod

Eventually I drummed up enough courage to share my struggles with Preston. We talked a lot about my dilemma but weren't able to come up with a viable solution. I went so far as to ask him to put locks in the wine refrigerator and solid teak liquor cabinet, which he did.

Sure, I continued my volunteer work in the hospital ministry, which I love and continue to this day—but it wasn't helping me meet and make new friendships. I wasn't drinking 24/7, seven days a week, and neither of us thought it was bad enough for me to enter a rehab facility.

All of my closest friends live an hour away in different directions, and are still working. It was impossible to get together during the week, and especially my weekends were devoted 100% to my man. Now that he's retired, he's all mine all the time and I love it!

If you've ever had a best friend, and lost them for a significant period of your life due to a misunderstanding you each couldn't get past (especially if you're a woman), you know how devastating it can be.

A few years after I remarried for the last time, my best friend broke up with me on FaceBook. I was so emotionally needy, feeling like a fish out of water in my new neighborhood, lonely and isolated from all that was familiar to me. The new friendships I tried so hard to form, were impossible to find.

She had recently remarried herself, a lovely man with four kids. Not only was she now a new wife after many years as a Christian divorcee, she was also stepmother to all these kids in addition to being a mom to her own.

Her new husband, a successful business owner, was excited to have her help him out, and she was happy to do so. What she didn't realize at the time, was what all this entailed. My dear, sweet friend was under pressure in all directions, and my whining about her being unable to come over and play now and then was more than she could bear.

Looking back, I absolutely don't blame her. OH, how I ached, and cried in my home office, morning, noon but never at night, because I didn't want to upset Preston. He would have felt responsible, when he was not, no matter how much I reassured him it's no one's fault, and that I'd never not once regret marrying him. I never have, and I never will.

She wasn't my only close friend by any stretch—I'm blessed to have five TRUE friends, all of which I have known for anywhere from 25-46 years; friends, to this day. But this particular friend was a fellow single mom, member of my church and lived 10 minutes away. We did everything together and have supported each other through it all. Losing her as an active daily participant in my life, was like losing the sun.

Sometimes—from a worldly perspective—a person can have everything anyone could ever possibly want, yet have very little of what truly matters. That was me, during this season of life. I'm a people person, and it was very difficult for me to not have close, personal friends nearby. Thankfully years later God reunited me with my old friend in a magnificent and unexpected way.

I saw my doctor about my insomnia, and she prescribed Ambien, which worked like a charm. Until it didn't. Preston became concerned about me, because I would do things in the middle of the night and not remember them the next day. He never shared his concerns with me to embarrass me, but he was very worried. And obviously after my accident at the lake, Ambien was out of my life forever.

Stopping taking Ambien, which absolutely helped me fall asleep, meant drinking more. I would go several days without sleeping, before I would break down from exhaustion and drink to help me fall asleep. You just can't know how harmful it is to a person when they don't sleep for days on end. Check out the *Huberman Podcast* to learn more.

The neural feedback loop my brain was running on was like this: I drank to fall asleep, it helped, so my brain developed a strong neural pathway to remember this as the solution. When I woke up a few hours later, I would just drink, without pausing to think about it. The drinking became automatic. Total nightmare. It was as if I had no brain at all. Unless and until I interrupted the cycle I wasn't even aware of at the time, the neural pathways would become stronger. The more I drank, the more I hated myself, the more I hated myself, and the more I drank to numb my feelings.

Eventually when I wasn't sleeping during the day, I discovered that alcohol was good for something else: numbing my feelings of boredom and isolation. In addition to being an 'effective' sleep aid, alcohol became my comforter. It listened to me and comforted me by taking away my emotional pain. I numbed out, and not being able to feel anything, felt better than continuing to feel like a loser because nothing was working.

My brain was continuing to rewire itself in a bad way, and I found myself drinking alcohol for whatever ailed me. It's like an old 45 record being played with a scratch on it. The song gets 'caught' on the same note over and over and over, never able to move to the next one unless it's turned off all together. The more I drank over time, the deeper the neural pathways became.

It sure would have helped to have understood these things from a neurological perspective back then, but I just assumed I was a loser drug user kind of person because no matter how hard I tried and wanted to, I could not stop drinking on my own for any length of time, years ago. My addiction to alcohol had nothing to do with being weak-willed and everything to do with my brain operating exactly as it was created to do. Period.

It Took Years to Escape

Around eight years ago I accompanied Preston on a business trip to California. While he attended the conference each day, I went sight-seeing. I took a tour of the infamous Alcatraz prison located on a small island just off the California coastline with the Golden Gate Bridge in plain sight.

What a cold, damp and claustrophobic place it was on the inside where the cells were. The tour guide showed us the cells the most infamous prisoners of all were kept, and where they clawed holes in the walls as one of the first steps in planning their big escape.

I felt like I was in the Alcatraz prison of alcohol, only without cellmates. It was just me, desperate to get out.

Like so many hundreds of thousands of people with AUD, not only were healthy coping skills and loving relationships not modeled for me by my parents, I also experienced years of childhood trauma, a/k/a adverse child experiences (AEC) that continued on through much of my adult life beginning with the murder of my dad, being raped as a 19-yr old virgin and keeping silent for decades, marrying two wrong men, sexual harassment in the workplace, etc.

The Center for Disease Control and Prevention (CDC)'s *CDC Vital Signs Adverse Childhood Experiences (ACEs)* report defines AECs as "potentially traumatic events that occur in children ages 0-17 years. The *CDC-Kaiser Permanente Adverse Childhood Experiences Study* says there are 10 types of childhood trauma children under the age of 18 may experience. According to the *AcesTooHigh* website, I scored 7 out of 10. Please Google the website if interested.

Why is this important? Because adults who have experienced a significant number of AECs are prone to developing addictions and/or substance use disorders, according to the CDC. Things did not bode well for me.

While I know my mom was traumatized as a child, since being abandoned by her father at a young age, as a grown woman now, I know she probably had no idea what her neglect was doing to me. A child's mind truly is like a movie-in-the-making. Everything he or she hears and sees creates neural pathways in the brain. The more repeated an experience becomes, the deeper the neural highway becomes.

Following are excerpts from a letter I wrote to my mom on Nov. 14, 1993, that may shed light on how damaging my ACEs were on me as a child. It's always important to note I don't share any of my personal experiences from a victim-mentality. Those who know me well, would be the first to tell you the last thing I would ever consider myself to be is a victim.

What prompted this letter to my mom was an incident that will remain private out of respect for her. While writing this book and reading my personal journals, when I found a copy of it. As I read it, my heart broke over how much it must have hurt her. But at the time, she needed to have her eyes opened and learn some things about her youngest daughter.

"... I'm going to hurt you deeply with this letter, but Mother, if we're ever going to have the kind of relationship I'm STARVING for, I must now talk—and you must now listen. I have been taking a class at church called "Making Peace with Your Past—Help for Adult Children of Dysfunctional Families." The characteristics of a dysfunctional family are as follows:

- A family member focusing its attention on an emotionally-needed family member.

- A family placing limits on the expression of feelings.

- A family discouraging open talk about obvious feelings.

- A family permitting destructive roles for the children in the family.

- A family failing to provide appropriate nurture for developing children.

- A family closed to the outside world.

"Although it may sound like I'm blaming you and Daddy for all we've been through—I'm not. I know you both did the best you could at the time, and neither of your parents' modeled healthy behavior to you and your siblings. Nevertheless, if we don't look at how we got here and talk about it, we'll never be able to heal, going forward.

"I have never felt loved by you, because you never expressed it in any way. I have never heard

"I love you" or "I'm so proud of you". Do you remember the many poems I used to write, including the one I saved my babysitting money for to place one in the newspaper for Mother's Day?

"I vividly remember the times Daddy would try and gouge your eyes out or strangle you. All of us would be in your bedroom screaming, crying and scampering about like frightened puppies. One time Henry jumped on his back trying to make him stop, and Daddy threw him against the window unit air conditioner for doing so. I remember Henry sleeping in the hallway in front of your bedroom door so if Daddy came stumbling down the hallway in the dark in a drunken stupor, he could protect you. Tall order for a little boy around eight-nine years old.

"I remember Daddy urinating on himself in the bed, us having to remove his clothing and clean him up in the middle of the night. I remember the smell of his urine. But in spite of his shortcomings, Daddy always made sure I knew he loved me. He was affectionate, he verbalized his love and used to tell me he would have to "beat the boys away with a stick" when I grew up.

"In all fairness to you, I can understand why you started drinking and taking pills. Anything—anything—to ease your pain. I don't blame you for doing whatever you had to do to get through the day, day in and day out.

"Nevertheless, you became an alcoholic and drug addict. I remember the car wrecks every summer when drove home from taking us to Aunt Jane's for two weeks. My guess is this when you first started trying to kill yourself. It was always so scary to visit you in the hospital, seeing you bruised, bandaged, with your legs and arms held together by something frightening-sounding called "traction". How embarrassing and scary it was, never knowing whose house we would be farmed out to while you recovered.

"Do you remember me standing next to you at the stove, crying because I didn't feel good? You kept telling me to be quiet; that is until I threw up everywhere. Only when you felt my burning forehead did you scream for Daddy to come here.

"Do you remember when we were at Aunt Jane's one summer? It was she, Uncle Greg, you and I on the patio overlooking the lake. With their house high on the hill, I'll never forget how pretty the view was. During this visit, y'all were heavily drinking. You and Aunt Jane went to the store and left me with Uncle Greg. He had me sit on his lap, and I felt something very hard against my thigh. I didn't know what it was, but I was very scared so I got up and told him I was going to look for arrowheads.

"I was perhaps 11 years old at the time, and walked down the hill by myself and began walking along the road. I wanted to try and find my way back to their house and go inside from the front. The longer I walked, the curvier the road became and I realized I was lost. My imagination had snakes and mountain lions rushing towards me and all I could do was cry. I know I was gone for several hours because the sun was going down. Thankfully you and Aunt Jane found me. I still remember the smell of liquor on your breaths.

"... the REAL reason I quit college was because I was raped the night of my 19th birthday by a fellow classmate I trusted. I couldn't tell anyone so I checked myself into the university clinic and was treated for depression ...

" ... I can't count the number of times over the coming years my siblings and I would get a call from the emergency room saying you'd tried to commit suicide again. The last time you did this, you really almost succeeded. We were never so scared in all of our lives, but we'd at the same time, had it with you. We were grown adults trying to raise our kids, keep jobs, etc. and were intensely angry. I can't remember who said it, but they told you if you really wanted to kill yourself, they'd bring you a gun so you could do it.

" ... I just want you to understand why we all literally cringe at the sound of your voice on the phone. Are you going to be coherent or so drunk we can barely understand your thick-tongued slurs?

" ... More than anything, I want you to love me. I want to love you again, and for you to love me. Mother, I AM sorry for having to share this letter with you, but I couldn't live with the remorse, guilt and pain if—years from now after you're gone—I realize I never had the guts to do so, and ruined any chance of having a real relationship with you.

" ... Please leave me alone for the time being. No calls, emails, no manipulating my siblings my trying to speak to me through them. I forgive you for everything, but I need some time to heal. I love you."

HOW GRATEFUL I AM that although it took a few weeks, we formed a new, real relationship based on authenticity and love. Although we didn't get nearly enough years together to enjoy it before she passed unexpectedly, I'm so very happy for both of us for the times we had together, going forward. Sadly, she continued playing with the demons of alcohol and pain pills until she passed away, but I focus now on the good memories rather than the bad.

The Fight of My Life

In this section I'm going to share all the many things I tried on my own to find freedom, the goal being to show how hard it was for me to do. I have tried so many things that it's impossible to remember the order in which these steps were taken, but I'll do my best to do so.

If my family ever reads this book, no one will ever be able to accuse me of not trying to overcome this nightmare. I believe I would have swam through a lake of alligators, if it would have taken this away from me. I believe I would have laid in a bed of snakes crawling over me, if it would have taken this away from me. Surely by now you understand how much I wanted to be healed.

1 Corinthians 3:13 states "Now these three remain are faith, hope and love, but the greatest of these is love." I'm sure my family loves me enough that if and when they read this, they will appreciate that I'm not who I used to be, I am indeed a new creation in Christ Jesus.

Hopefully, they would all be filled with compassion and respect that I suffered silently not wanting to resurrect painful memories of our childhood and young adulthood, and admire my perseverance in following every step put in front of me.

As I'm writing this, I can clearly see that God allowed me to go through all these steps as a way to prove to me and anyone reading this, that really, all we need to do is go to Him, first. For everything. At all times. I wasted so much time, energy, emotion and wishing I wouldn't wake up in the mornings, all to no avail.

Trust me when I say—JUST GO TO GOD with your problems, FIRST. Always! Like the prodigal son, it took years for me to come to my senses and only then, with the help of a trusted pastor and longtime friend.

With chronic insomnia being the sole reason for my brain attaching to alcohol as a solution, it was important to me to try and get it under control while at the same time, trying to solve the alcohol puzzle.

My insomnia got so bad that I saw three doctors simultaneously for almost two years: my primary care physician, a board-certified sleep specialist and a cognitive behavior therapist who specialized in treating insomnia.

Together they created a strict sleep regimen. While it helped to some degree, eventually it stopped being as effective. Short of taking drastic measures like Michael Jackson did years ago (which I would NEVER do), I accepted that this would be a lifelong thorn in my side, waiting for God to answer my prayers regarding sleep.

Having said that, following are some of the many things I tried to free myself from the addiction. It shouldn't surprise you what the first step was. LOL

Alcoholics Anonymous, a/k/a "AA"

Years before my accident, the first thing I did to try and stop drinking on my own, was attend AA meetings. Having attended Al-Anon meetings as a child, I recalled having memories—more or less—about what I learned regarding the 12 Steps of AA. After the meeting I walked up the aisle of shame for the first of 10-million times to accept my 24-hour chip, thus admitting I was an "alcoholic". Attaching this label to myself felt about as right as drinking alcohol to cure insomnia. It was wrong, and I knew it, but I also didn't know anything else at the time.

By Googling "Am I an Alcoholic", you'll find loads of links to questionnaires to help you answer some questions, but they also include disclaimers being unable to properly diagnose you for alcoholism. Only you can decide if you're an alcoholic. Why is alcoholism the only disease I must diagnose for myself? I find it so absurd. It didn't make sense to me then, and it doesn't, now. Nevertheless, this was all I knew at the time.

My sponsor was an older woman, and while I would like to say she was just lovely; she wasn't. Her immediate disappointment in my first relapse would play like a broken record in my head when I let it. "YOU—of ALL PEOPLE—*with the power of the Holy Spirit living inside of you* should be able to put down that drink and keep it down!

Steps 1-3 of AA says one is to admit they are powerless over alcohol, be convinced something greater than themselves is able to help, and submit to a power they believe is higher than themselves. Hek, I graduated with honors on these first three steps the morning I came forward at my brother's church and accepted God's free gift of salvation, years earlier.

Although she was right, I still wasn't able to put the glass down. The guilt, shame and self-loathing increased ten-fold after this, and I distinctly recall when I went to bed that night, letting God know I was 100-percent OK if He wanted to go ahead and call me home, so to speak. Her judgment and condemnation only made me feel worse, which of course led me to drink more to numb out those painful emotions.

It makes me sad to admit how often I used to pray that I would just wake up in heaven so I wouldn't have the mental, emotional, spiritual and physical torment I lived with 24/7. While it may sound like I was suicidal, I would *never* take my own life.

On the outside, my life was a sunny day and I always had a smile on my face, but inside a dark spiritual battle was going on. I wish I would have known that's what it was at the time. I should have, but the truth is, I didn't. I was just tired of fighting with myself, unable to understand why this happened— how it happened—and most importantly, how to escape the prison cell my mind had become.

Eventually I found a second sponsor, a truly lovely, humble Christian woman who worked with me through the 12 steps for well over a year. I tried so hard. And kept failing.

Although my periods of sobriety *were lengthening*, I have learned since then that sobriety *isn't* just about never putting alcohol into your mouth again as long as you live. *It's equally if not more-so valuable about learning healthy coping skills, handling one's emotions from one minute to the next*, because life can quickly change.

Celebrate Recovery

The next step I tried was joining Celebrate Recovery, a Christ-centered 12-step program at a local church. Again, please don't misunderstand me. The 12 steps of both AA and Celebrate Recovery are wonderful, and are a great blueprint for anyone's life whether they struggle with any type of addiction or not.

I followed them and did the program to the best of my ability. For me, back then, it wasn't helpful, long-term. I think I kept thinking I would be able to live as a 'normal drinker' one day. And from what I know now about alcohol, even if I COULD go back to drinking 'normally', there's no way I ever would. I don't WANT it. *FREEDOM!*

Medication was Useless

Through listening to one of many podcasts, I learned about Naltrexone, a prescription medication approved by the Food and Drug Administration (FDA) to treat AUD and addictions in general. The non-addictive medication blocks both the stimulant ('buzz') and depressant (sedative) effects by binding and blocking certain receptors in the brain, thus reducing and/or suppressing cravings. It didn't work for me, but at least I gave it a go.

Various Forms of Therapy:

I was open to all kinds of therapy, including the Emotional Freedom Technique ("EFT"), a/k/a tapping. EFT is a form of therapy created for people suffering from post-traumatic stress disorder (PTSD), anxiety and other mental health disorders. While I don't have PTSD or anxiety, I most definitely have a degree in ACEs. LOL.

Gary Craig, EFT's creator, believes tapping on different parts of the body while speaking to oneself about what they're feeling helps reduce physical and emotional pain and re-balance energy. When you're as desperate as I was to find a solution, you'll try anything. And while it didn't help me, many people in my online support group have had great success with it. There are apps to help you along.

Next, I tried Eye Movement Desensitization and Reprocessing (EMDR) therapy. This is believed to help people heal from long-internalized pain from difficult traumatic life experiences.

Patients' whose brains have been thrown out of whack as the result of a challenging experience, left untreated, the emotional wounds will fester, causing intense suffering that manifests in even more harmful ways.

Especially for adults who were never shown or taught healthy coping skills, as I obviously never was, I was desperate to try anything and continued to do so. EMDR was helpful to me to process my sexual assault and understand the poor choices I made as a young woman as a result, but it didn't help solve the alcohol puzzle.

My primary care physician referred me to a regular, run-of-the-mill therapist. Fortunately for me, she was also a Christian, so it was extremely helpful for me to talk about things from a Biblical perspective. I was devastated to learn she was resigning, but very happy for the veterans with PTSD she would be serving in her new position.

Throughout the years this battle has entailed, in many ways and as weird as it sounds, I learned to re-parent myself. I framed a small photo of myself when I was six years old and put it next to my computer, at the suggestion of my therapist. While doing the work therapy and counseling requires, I would look over at six-year-old self with love and a heart of compassion for all I have been through, most of which I was not responsible for.

I reminded myself I had no choice in who my parents would be or what kind of family I would grow up in, any more than my siblings did. I gave myself the same compassion I would give to anyone I came across with this level of pain and suffering. I can't remember how this idea was introduced to me, and laugh all you want but it was helpful.

Part of my shame-based distorted views of myself were steeped in what I call the 'not good enough' syndrome that began when I was a young child. I believed I wasn't good enough for my own mother because of how she did and didn't treat me.

My hearing problems added to my belief that something was wrong with me. With society's continual intense pressure to be thin, I definitely struggled with my weight all my life, and even unto this day. The sexual assault ripped my soul in two, causing so much shame and cemented fully and completely, that I was damaged goods and would be lucky if any man gave me the time of day. I think I'm in some ways allowing myself to remain overweight so no one will look at me. How sad; I need to look at this, more.

Two failed marriages (especially the second one, which was abusive), endless broken hearts, not having a college degree which led me to believe I wasn't good enough to make it as a real journalist, etc. all contributed to me not feeling worthy of anyone or anything, for that matter. To this day, I can still hear the constant criticisms of one man in particular, if something triggers me.

No wonder I needed God so much. No wonder He is and always has been, my all-in-all, the only true Source for everything. I lost my way for a time out of pride, stupidity, and believing the enemy's lies. That is the truth. Is it your truth, too? If so, remember that faith, what you **KNOW** about God, *trumps* how you <u>feel</u>.

Another step my therapist recommended was to write letters to my parents—and myself—forgiving all of us for all the things. Although they were long since passed away, it was very helpful for me.

Lest you find yourself wondering why I didn't run to the nearest church, let me ask you: when was the last time AUD/alcoholism (whatever term you prefer) was preached from the pulpit? I believe there may be many of my brothers and sisters in Christ—just like me—who find themselves drinking way more than they ever intended, and find themselves drowning in the same guilt, shame and self-loathing.

If we are to fulfill God's call upon our lives, we need help from the church at large. God's Word tells us that all things hidden will come to light, so for heaven's sakes let's be reminded by our pastors about the forgiveness available to us and reminders to those who don't suffer from this particular condition, that they too have their own 'conditions'—and they know it. We're all sinners in need of a Savior.

One time I asked someone what their biggest sin was, and they said they didn't think they had any. I wanted to laugh and point out that pride is a sin, and one of the ones God hates the most. I should have referenced 1 John 1:8, which says, "If we say we have no sin we are deceiving ourselves, and the truth is not in us." Anyway, I digress.

I finally found the courage to confess my sins to one of my elderly pastor friends at church.

When I did so, he immediately said, "I have been clean and sober for 20 years." What relief that brought me. He recommended a Biblical counselor and fellow church member, so reaching out to her was the next thing I did.

Over the course of almost a year, Jackie and I worked through *The Heart of Addiction* and its accompanying workbook by Mark E. Shaw. This book burst my broken heart to emotional shrapnel, because it tapped into my relationship with God and reminded me of just how far I'd strayed from Him during recent years.

As He is so faithful to do, God gave me the gift of repentance and I laid myself bare to the best of my ability. Although I knew my sins were forgiven since the day I accepted Christ in the 1990s, I cried off and on for weeks and months on end. He spoke to me during this time, comforting me and letting me know He was going to lead me out of this hell-hole in His perfect ways and in His perfect timing.

Although God didn't create this trial by fire—I was responsible for it—He encouraged me by saying He was going to turn it around for my good, the good of others, and His glory, as is His promise found in Romans 8:28.

Once Jackie felt I was steady on my feet, we agreed to part ways, knowing her number was in my phone and I could call on her at any time. Which I should have done but didn't do when life became challenging again for one reason or another. Much like a baby learning to walk and continuing to fall and get back up, I was still learning. This was a fall; another costly mistake to add to my collection of falls.

<u>Books, Podcasts and Online Programs</u>:

Before too long I discovered the *30-Day Sobriety Solution* book and accompanying online program. I learned a lot of good information, but obviously it didn't stick; however, it doesn't mean this or any other book/programs haven't worked or won't work for other people.

At some point I stumbled upon a Kindle ad for *This Naked Mind*, by Annie Grace. The title intrigued me and once I read what it was about, I quickly downloaded it. Never have I ever felt so understood, calmed down and at the same time excited by a book as when I plowed through this one. To date I have read it about six times.

Annie found freedom from alcohol through unconventional means and was ready to help others do so. Like me—like hundreds of thousands of people worldwide—she needed to understand what she was dealing with in order to gain the upper hand.

Once she created a podcast under the same name, I was hooked on listening to stories from countless other people from all walks of life, and began to have hope that her unique methods for helping people regain control of their relationship with alcohol or make the decision to quit drinking all together, would work for me as long as I didn't give up trying.

Through the next several years I began reading every book I could find on alcohol, addiction in general and AUD, and expanded my library of not only God-honoring podcasts to help me grow in my Christian faith and encourage my goal of sobriety.

When life became unmanageable again and I started drinking off and on, I joined another online program, this one offered by Annie Grace. I was asked to create a list of why I thought I wanted to drink, what its perceived benefits were, and why I wanted to stop drinking. By learning to challenge my beliefs one at a time, it was easier to reduce the amount I drank, and the periods between having drinks were getting longer and longer.

The program was brilliant because it required me to dig deep within myself and ask why I believed alcohol helped me to sleep, when upon further reflection, I realized it actually wreaked havoc on my sleep. More on this in Chapter 7—The Truth About Alcohol. I also thought alcohol helped me relax in social situations, when in fact it only increased my anxiety a few drinks in because my body and brain were being negatively affected.

I took a course entitled *The Addictive Brain* by Professor Thad A. Polk, University of Michigan, and continued doing my own research through trusted healthcare and government websites. Polk's work on neuroplasticity reinforced my confidence and self-esteem, giving me hope that with God's help I could and would rewire my dang brain and get back to my normal self again.

Why do I find this utterly fascinating? Because remember, God is the Creator of all things, *including* science. God's Word tells us to transform and renew our minds, which we do by reading and meditating on it. This is also known as neuroplasticity.

Remember earlier when I mentioned telling Preston I *knew* my brain had changed? Well, *I know my brain has changed again* and is whole and healed from the damage caused by alcohol. I know this, like I know God loves me.

Connection is Key

One of the biggest missing links to stopping drinking and staying stopped, I learned, was the power of connection with others who shared the same fight. Although Preston and other family members and friends love me, the majority of them have no idea how long I have suffered from this, how hard I have tried to regain my true life back, nor do most of them know what it's like to have this particular nightmare.

The friendships I have formed with my fellow classmates have played a big part in helping me find freedom from alcohol prison, one day at a time. Before the program ended, a private Marco Polo group was formed so we could stay in touch via video messaging. A calendar was created with a private Zoom link for daily Zoom calls with whoever wants to join. I host the Saturday morning calls and look forward to them each week. Finally, someone created a private BAND group (similar to FaceBook).

I can't begin to tell you how much this online support family means to me. Lest you think people who develop addictions to alcohol and/or AUD are losers, in my group we have a (in no particular order) stay-at-home moms, real estate professionals, a successful retired business owner, a retired corporate airline pilot, a couple of doctors, a nurse practitioner, several nurses (retired and active), teachers (active and retired), an artist, etc.

And guess what? Since this wasn't the first online program I had taken, and wasn't the first online community I'd been a part of, I can tell you that the other communities were also comprised of equally-impressive intelligent people who also developed problems with alcohol. The drug doesn't discriminate, and it has absolutely <u>nothing</u> to do with whether or not someone is a "good person". Stop judging us! LOL. "Judge not, lest you be judged," says Matthew 7:1!

"My people" and I are bonded in a way none of us ever thought possible. Many are fellow believers, some aren't—but we are all equally loved, valued, admired and respected. I have seen some of them go through some hard times that I believe are leading them to consider turning to God, perhaps for the first time.

God created us to be in fellowship with one another, especially during life's biggest challenges. Addiction needs someone to be isolated and feeling terrible about themselves in order to thrive. By staying connected to Him and returning to the practices I used to do as a new believer more than 30 years ago, and remaining in touch daily with these beautiful souls He's brought together, I have walked out of alcohol prison and given Him the key. For real.

<u>Other Lessons Learned</u>

I learned how to handle life's hard knocks and pain of every type by using healthy coping skills, and today I can honestly say I have absolutely no desire to drink whatsoever. Because alcohol offers nothing but misery, I experience no more temptation, triggers or cravings. I have learned to follow the storyline in my head, always remembering that if I were to drink again, how it always ends badly.

But do you want to know what the number one REAL SECRET of my Spirit-led sobriety is? **Every morning when I wake up and have quiet time with God, I thank Him for helping me stay out of prison yesterday, and ask Him to please help me stay out of prison again, today.**

As a little girl, one of my fondest memories of my dad was when we slow-danced together. I would stand on his feet while he held me close, swayed me across the room and whispered such tender words of life to me. "My sweet Paulette. Never forget you can do anything you put your mind to." Now as a 65-year old woman, I stand on my heavenly Father's feet, dancing with Him as He speaks sweet truth to me.

God and only God, remaining close to Him, HE is my solution now. For everything. Always and forever.

Overcome Cognitive Dissonance by Renewing Your Mind

What was really going down in my mind was from a science-based perspective was cognitive dissonance. As a reminder, the *Merriam-Webster Dictionary* defines cognitive dissonance as the "psychological conflict resulting from having incongruous beliefs and attitudes simultaneously".

If you've ever had a strong craving for your favorite dessert, but you're on a diet and know you'd blow it by having it, there's a mental tug-of-war happening. This is cognitive dissonance.

Welcome to my former life.

While giving into enjoying your craving for dessert, it won't kill you, ruin your health, diminish your cognitive abilities or the ability to form memories, etc. People with addictions and substance abuse disorder of any type aren't as fortunate.

Many if not most people suffering from AUD and/or addictions of any type will tell you cognitive dissonance feels like a literal battle in your mind. Satan's voice was constantly telling me, "Oh go ahead just one won't hurt you've been so good no one will ever know you don't have a problem everyone's doing it you can too" on a non-stop repeat loop. This is neural feedback loop Dr. Helmstetter described in *The Power of Neuroplasticity*.

Even when I worked up days, weeks and months of sobriety, seemingly suddenly and out of nowhere, he would push the 'play' button and the incessant loop would play over and over and over again. And even then, again.

Every time I heard what I NOW know was Satan's voice, it helped to visualize that androgynous character from Mel Gibson's movie, *Passion of the Christ*, years ago. To me the way this pathetic but powerful foe was portrayed in that movie as neither man nor woman, gave me the heebie jeebies, and I knew it was definitely not on my side.

You may be comforted from knowing that the apostle Paul suffered from cognitive dissonance. Check it out:

For the good that I want, I do not do, but I practice the very evil that I do not want. But if I am doing the very thing I do not want, I am no longer the one doing it, but sin which dwells in me.
—Romans 7:14-15

Unless we learn to transform and renew our minds from the inside out and eliminate the cognitive dissonance once and for all, every day is like that of Bill Murray's character in the movie, "Groundhog Day". A total nightmare.

OH how I wish I had known years ago, the voice in my head that kept telling me it was OK to have another drink, I 'needed it', was actually Satan causing such havoc. I would have known right away how to fight back, by speaking God's Word out loud over my life and praying in faith, regardless of how much I hated myself and hoped many times I just wouldn't wake up the next day. That seemed so easier than fighting this invisible war that no one knew I was fighting but me.

I'd wake up hours later unable to fall back asleep, and the guilt, shame and worst of all, self-loathing machine kicked in. Oh, how hopeless and helpless I used to feel. And what did I do when these bad feelings rose up? Considering healthy coping skills to deal with unpleasant emotions and experiences were never not once taught to me by my parents or anyone else, I drank to numb them and check out for a few more hours. I didn't know what else to do, back then.

Another example of what happens when someone with a substance use disorder or addiction, is they'll be fine one minute, and without any real reason, trigger or craving—they will suddenly find themselves with a drink in their hands. They weren't even thinking about drinking, and here they are doing it.

I know—I Know—I KNOW this doesn't sound believable nor does it make sense. I'm writing this book out of obedience to God, so trust me—I'm not lying or exaggerating with this example. It is as shocking to us as it is for a newborn baby leaving the dark, cozy womb of its mother and finding itself in a cold, harsh light.

The apostle Paul reveals the hope we have in Christ Jesus:

... but I see a different law in the members of my body, waging war against the law of my mind and making me a prisoner of the law of win which is in my members. Wretched man that I am! Who will set me free from the body of this death? Thanks be to God through Jesus Christ our Lord! So then, on the one hand I myself with my mind am serving the Law of God, but on the other, with my flesh the law of sin. THEREFORE there is now no condemnation for those who are in Christ Jesus. For the law of the Spirit of life in Christ Jesus has set you free from this law of sin and death.
—Romans 7:23-8:1-2

God calls us to transform and renew our minds from the inside out. Because I had fallen away from my first Love—not realizing it at the time—is it any wonder Satan found so an easy entry into my mind?

Rather than turning to God for help with everything that bothered me, starting with the blasted insomnia, I discovered alcohol was an effective solution for many of my problems; until it became THE biggest problem I'd ever faced in my life.

Who are you going to listen to when faced with a problem? Someone who's had it and lived to tell the tale, or someone who has no experience and as much as they want to help, they can't?

For we do not have a high priest who is unable to sympathize with our weaknesses, but we have one who has been tempted in every way, just as we are—yet was without sin. Let us then approach the throne of grace with confidence, so that we may receive mercy and find grace to help us in our time of need.—Hebrews 4:15-16

In my anguish I cried to the Lord, and He answered me by setting me free.
—Psalm 118:5

I spent so much time in prayer and remembered the things I used to do years ago when I first became a believer that helped me draw closer to God.

One of those things was to read through Scripture verses that the Holy Spirit led me to, put them out into a Word document and laminate it to pray from every morning. We know God's Word spoken out loud will defeat every enemy this side of heaven, every time. I know this **for a fact** in my own life because this is a fail-proof strategy that has worked <u>for over 30 years for me</u>.

When out walking or running errands, I began listening to and singing praise and worship songs—another winning method. It's hard to hate yourself when you're worshiping God!

WHAT TOOK MY THICK SKULL so freaking long to get it? I'll tell you what I think. I believe it was my pride and ego.

E—Edging

G   God

O—Out

That's what egos do, in my humble opinion and personal experience. But here's another thing I have learned along my years of fighting this war: Whether or not I'm at fault for becoming addicted to alcohol, slowing its progression to that of AUD before finally being delivered, whether or not God allowed Satan to test me in THE absolute hardest life experience I have ever endured, it doesn't matter—He is going to use this escape from alcohol prison to help anyone who needs it, and I believe this book is just one tool He has brought forth to do so. Otherwise, why would He ask me to write it?

As we spend time in God's Word, through prayer and meditation, He indeed transforms and renews our minds from the inside out. "I believe that our neural pathways can be made new by Him as we live in new habit patterns," said Mark Shaw, author of *The Heart of Addiction* and *RELAPSE.* "I believe He enables our bodies to be renewed in order that we might live for Him and His glory, thereby enjoying the fruit of His Spirit that Galatians [5:22] talks about."

Slowly but surely, I began to notice significant progress. Knowing what I know now, I would venture to say I had gone from being addicted to alcohol, to at this point having mild AUD. I went weeks and months at a time without drinking, then something would trigger me and I would have alcohol just the one night. But the one night would be followed by a several day binge, before I would get it back under control and not drink again for months on end.

It was only through God's help and perseverance that I was able to finally receive His deliverance of this nightmare one day at a time. That saying, 'one day at a time', is the only thing AA-related that resonates with me. And it makes sense because Jesus Himself reminds us not to worry about tomorrow because tomorrow will take care of itself.

My New, Best Life

What I want everyone to know, is how much better life is on the other side of the prison walls. Once you are freed—stay freed. Everything about my life—my faith, relationships, health, energy level, peace of mind and self-confidence—have improved from night-to-day. I would venture to say I'm finally the woman God created me to be, as if I had never had a drink of alcohol in all my life.

Most importantly, I'm closer to God than I have ever been in my life, now. For this reason alone, I have learned to be grateful for the years of pain and suffering I have endured through my sinful choices as well as hard life experiences I never asked for.

Small Daily Steps That Help Me:

- Prayer, meditation, quiet time and journaling with God every morning, first thing in the morning. This includes praying Scripture verses out loud regarding whatever I'm needing help with at the time.
- Exercising
- Listening to and singing praise and worship songs and/or podcasts, usually while walking
- Online support family via BAND, Marco Polo and Zoom calls

- Scrolling through sober accounts on Instagram
- Remembering my list of 'why's'
- Playing the tape forward (how will this end?)
- Reminding myself how I'll feel tomorrow, especially on an emotional level, if I were to drink again.
- Keeping some alcohol-free wine and spirits to have on hand when I'm feeling triggered or experiencing FOMO (fear of missing out). While this has been helpful for many, I have only had one glass of alcohol-free wine while visiting friends out of town. I have never opened the alcohol-free spirits in the cabinet in the kitchen. I honestly don't want alcohol anymore.
- Volunteering at my church when needed.

Chapter 7

The Truth about Alcohol

In March 2023, the JAMA Network Open released a new analytic study from more than 40 years of research that concluded moderate drinking offers no protection whatsoever against heart disease, nor does it contribute to a longer life, as previously thought for many years.

The research study followed almost 400,000 people and concluded that even low alcohol intake actually *increased* a risk of disease and death. 'Relatively low levels of alcohol' meant less than 1 ounce of alcohol for women and about 1.5 ounces or more per day for men, according to the study. In the US, the standard drink is 5 ounces of wine, 12 ounces of beer or 1.5 ounces of distilled spirits.

In terms of health, less alcohol is better, according to Tim Naimi, author of the study and director of the Canadian Institute for Substance

Use research and professor of public health and society policy at the University of Victoria.

Oh, how I wish there were never such a thing as alcohol to begin with. Think of the millions of lives, marriages and families that would be saved. More importantly, consider that God has given each of us unique set of abilities and talents to be used for the good of others, and His glory.

I can think of nothing sadder than lives, not well-lived, not fulfilling God's purposes for them. Can you just imagine living in a world where everyone knew what their gifts and talents were, developed them over time, serving others while providing for themselves and their families? I can.

But the enemy of our souls knows just where our weak spots are, and zooms in for the kill by alluring us with false promises that alcohol is just what we need to cure our boo-boos. What a lie, straight from the pits of hell.

Recently I began noticing the vision in my left eye was blurry, so I went to the eye doctor and received a new Rx for new eyeglasses. I decided to opt for progressive lenses that allow you to view things up close and at a distance simultaneously, depending on the angle I was viewing them through. In addition, I thought the transitional technology was a great idea, as it eliminated the need for sunglasses. When I go outside, the lenses automatically become dark within seconds; and, when I come inside, they become clear again.

When I began to learn from research that my brain functions had literally changed because of excessive drinking of alcohol for the wrong reasons over long periods of time—that if I drank, I no longer had an 'off' switch—I knew I needed help. I needed to understand why and how this happened and began searching for answers.

Just as the way my new glasses help me see things as they truly are, the more I researched alcohol and looked for answers, my eyes began to open and see the truth behind what I'd allowed myself to consume.

The liquid we've been drinking—whether its beer, wine or hard spirits—is ethanol. Yes, THAT ethanol. We've been consuming a flammable liquid. The same exact ethanol we fill our gas tanks with, only in a much smaller percentage and with enough additives by the manufacturers to make it somewhat palatable. I know, I know it's hard to believe. Google it for yourself, as I did.

Alcohol was never meant to become a recreational drug, but it was used years ago as an anesthetic during times of war. The National Toxicology Program of the US Department of Health and Human Services' *"Report on Carcinogens"* states alcohol is a known carcinogen. The seven types of cancer alcohol may cause include head and neck cancer, esophageal cancer, liver cancer and breast cancer.

Drinking alcohol to cope with stress, physical or emotional pain, boredom, loneliness or any other common ailments of the human condition—while providing relief temporarily—alcohol tends to enhance negative emotional states between drinking episodes. That's because alcohol acts as both a stimulant and a depressant.

Suddenly the "normal" drinker finds themselves chronically misusing, making it difficult if not impossible to control. Neural pathways in the brain literally change as a result of continual alcohol use over time. They may endure long after a person stops drinking and can contribute to relapses during their recovery.

I remember telling Preston something was wrong with me, that I no longer processed alcohol the same way. I knew something was different, I just didn't know why or how things became different. Or, just how hard it would be and long it would take to find a way of getting well.

What many people, including myself, usually do is judge others if and when they become addicted to alcohol or becoming an "alcoholic". Through researching for this book, I learned there are now two diagnoses instead of one.

Alcohol addiction is categorized by the NIAAA as "a chronic relapsing disorder associated with compulsive alcohol drinking, the loss of control over intake, and the emergence of a negative emotional state when alcohol is no longer available."

The *"Understanding Alcohol Use Disorder"* report by the NIAAA, described AUD as "a medical condition characterized by an impaired ability to stop or control alcohol use despite adverse social, occupational, or health consequences." Although both conditions sound similar, they are two separate diagnoses.

Whether or not a person develops AUD depends on many factors, including how much, how often and how quickly they consume alcohol, according to the NIAAA. The report went on to say genetics was responsible for about 60% of cases, and the risk for developing AUD increased by the interplay between a person's environment and their parents' drinking habits.

Professor Polk says while our genetic makeup can influence how susceptible some people may be to addiction, it proves we may be at risk. "We inherit two versions of each gene our parents, and apparently one or more of these genes can influence our susceptibility to addiction," he writes.

People suffering from post-traumatic stress disorder, depression and adverse child experiences (ACEs) were also at risk. Given everything I had gone through up until this time, I didn't stand a chance against this beast.

God's Perspective on Alcohol Misuse

The spiritual aspects of alcohol and the havoc it wreaks in a person's lives are viewed differently, as they should be. I can assure you and God knows I'm being honest when I say I had no intention of developing an addiction to alcohol, which began when I followed the advice of a well-meaning friend to try drinking alcohol to help me fall asleep.

I was desperate, it worked, and then I discovered it worked for a lot of other problems I had, until it didn't. I was a 'normal' (social) drinker for many decades without a problem, and I wasn't drinking to have fun anymore. I was taking the alcohol as I would a prescription offered by my doctor. Literally, for medicinal purposes. I was not catching a buzz, by any stretch of the imagination, at the time I realized I had a problem.

"There are certainly environmental factors (nurture) and genetic factors (nature) that impact addiction but I wouldn't say that these are CAUSAL. The cause is our fallen, broken and sinful state of being that seeks to serve ourselves as 'god' rather than the One True God," Shaw explained.

"When we live in this idolatrous way, we seek all kinds of 'tools (Isaiah 44:9-20) for idolatry that we use to carve out our idols of self. In other words, cocaine, marijuana, alcohol and heroin are simply tools that an idolater uses because the idolater is worshiping oneself. The tool is used because the idolater likes the way it makes him/her feel so in that way, it is metaphorically carving out the god of self," he continued.

Based on my personal experiences, observations and years of torment, I had no idea that so much drinking in an effort to sleep, as well as using it to numb painful emotions, led me to the sin of idolatry, in God's eyes. And until I was given the gift of repentance, I would have remained in such suffering.

In no way am I accusing anyone of committing the sin of idolatry as a result of or in addition to excessive consumption of alcohol. Again, I am no one's judge or jury. I myself was convicted that this was the root of the problem, the heart of my addiction, through reading Shaw's book and going through Biblical counseling. I'm definitely not proud of myself, but I take comfort in knowing God is a God of redemption and restoration.

"Satan encourages a seemingly good thing and we do it, and then we end up hating it because it enslaves us. We feel stuck and hopeless as if there is no escape, but God wants us to run to Him and draw near to His throne of grace," said Shaw, who has 28 years of sobriety.

You may be interested to know I spoke with three pastors on the condition of anonymity, as I was concerned about the possibility of this sin of drunkenness being a generational curse based on Old Testament readings. It sure seemed like a curse to me. None of them believed this to be the case, and I was greatly relieved to learn this.

For an in-depth education into the dangers and effects of alcohol, I recommend you check out the resources I have listed in Chapter 10. Specifically, listening to "What Alcohol Does to the Brain and Body", Episode 86 of the *Huberman Podcast*, reading *This Naked Mind* by Annie Grace and *Alcohol Explained* by William Porter.

Finally, alcohol is known to be an addictive drug. The World Health Organization estimated there are approximately 140 million people worldwide who are addicted to it.

Chapter 8

Alcohol Marketing

Come One, Come All—Taste the Most Dangerous, Drink of All! We proudly introduce to you, ethanol in a glass! With each sip, you're increasing your chances of ...

- Anxiety
- Depression
- Developing heart disease, stroke, high blood pressure, diabetes, weight gain and seven different types of cancer, among other things!
- Divorce
- Possible sexual assault
- Losing your kids
- Suicidal thoughts
- Hurting yourself or someone you love
- Losing your job, home and possible jail or even prison time!
- Losing your ability to make good decisions, protect yourself and your

loved ones in dangerous situations, and let's not forget your ability to remember things!

- It will undermine if not completely eliminate your confidence, courage, self-respect, reputation while developing a tolerance for it while addicting you at the same time. You'll be lining our pocketbooks with more money as you will need more of it as you try ever so valiantly to achieve the temporary buzz you initially felt!

- Physical, emotional and verbal reactions will be delayed, and you may do, say and write things you'll regret in the morning!

- Thanks to its dehydrating properties, you're almost guarantee to wake up with a pounding head ache because your blood is trying to pump through a dehydrated brain!

The list of benefits is just *endless*, so we thought we'd leave you with one last thought. By consuming our product, "Death in a Drink", you may even lose—wait for it—your LIFE!

"Drink Responsibly!"

Many if not most people drink alcohol to socialize, alleviate stress and anxiety, help them fall asleep, numb out feelings of boredom and loneliness, etc.

While going to the store this morning, I took photos of numerous wine bottles and various pieces of merchandise aimed at consumers of every age. We've all seen kitchen towels, coffee cups, wine glasses, wall plaques and t-shirts with funny slogans. Now that you know the truth—that alcohol is ethanol, a toxic poison humans were never created to consume—would you think this slogan I discovered on wine glasses is still cute?

"Because kids". With a wine glass above this slogan on a kitchen towel, think about what kind of message is this sending to moms. And more importantly, their kids. Could it be something like, 'I'm not strong enough to raise my children unless I'm drinking?' Or, 'My parents can't raise me without drinking?'

I don't know the answers to these questions I have posed. Do you? Is it time we start paying attention to what the world is selling us?

A Sampling of Additional Drinking Slogans

- Because work
- Drink happy thoughts
- Drunken grownups—America runs on wine
- Emotional support beverage
- I had to deal with people today
- It's fine I'm fine everything is fine
- Never too far to wine together
- Wine a little and laugh a lot
- You can't buy happiness, but you can buy wine and that's kind of the same thing

Lest anyone doubt Satan is drinking cocktails as marketing executives roll out name brands for up and coming vinos, check out below, the names on actual wine bottles I also took notice of while shopping. Make up your own mind about the spiritual connotations, and ask yourself how reading them makes you feel. What are they trying to promise you, here?

- Apothic Inferno
- Ava Grace
- New Age
- Prophecy
- Rapture
- Spellbound
- The Prisoner
- Uncaged
- Whispering Angel
- Z Deadly Zins

Now let's look at labels that may or may not appeal to egos, emotions and identities:

- Bar Dog
- Bread & Butter
- Decoy

- Educated Guess

- FitVine

- Freakshow

- Instigator

- Menage a Trois Decadence

- 19 Crimes

- Pessimist

- Sideshow—The Puppetmaster

- Stags Leap

- Storyteller

- The Federalist

- Uppercut

Can you see how these slogans and brand names may or may not appeal to the stressed out working mom with a screaming toddler in the grocery cart? The exhausted executive on his way home, depressed over his recent divorce? What about the hostess of a book club, wanting to fit in with her new neighbors? Young adults looking for "love" by wanting to offer a nightcap before that first date ends?

All is Not Lost

Because I have fought this fight for years, and am winning it day-by-day by the grace of God and my online friends, I have observed—not a seismic shift—but a gradual increase by the general population seeking to reduce or eliminate its consumption of alcohol.

Programs like Dry January, Feb Fast, Dry July and Sober October are on the rise. Once people take a break from alcohol for even just 30 days—if they can make it that long—many I personally know have experienced increased happiness and an overall sense of well-being, improved sleep, more money in their pockets, more energy and improved relationships, to name a few.

Dry bars are popping up all over the place, and people are enjoying clever-sounding mocktails (alcohol-free beverages). There is a growing market for alcohol-free wine and spirits, thanks in large part to millennials making up 48% of drinkers whose preference is low- or no-alcohol beer.

A non-alcohol Mindful Drinking Fest was held in Washington, DC in January 2023. All drinks were zero-proof, and the fact that it was sold out gives evidence that being alcohol-free is more than just a trend—it's entirely possible that it's here to stay. The 300+ attendees included locals, of course, but people from as far away as Colorado and Canada enjoyed the festivities. Vendors came in for the event from Florida, Oregon, California and the UK.

Another simply amazing sign of progress, one I NEVER thought possible, was just shared this very morning. One of my friends was at Gatwick Airport in London waiting for departure. While heading towards her gate, she stopped by one of the stores in the airport and was shocked to find a small section of alcohol-free beverages. When flights are delayed or canceled, and you're traveling alone, you're free to drink as much as you want without judgment, airports can just be a disaster.

Chapter 9

Warnings and Wisdom

God's Word truly is the best instruction manual for life and how to live our best lives on earth. Following are a sampling of Scriptures about alcohol, drunkenness, hope, healing and encouragement to help remind us why alcohol offers no benefits whatsoever and that with God, we can and will overcome this.

Wine is a mocker and beer a brawler; whoever is led astray by them is not wise.—Proverbs 20:1

But if we walk in the light as He Himself is in the light, we have fellowship with one another, and the blood of Jesus His Son cleanses us from all sin. —
1 John 1:7

*Listen, my son, and be wise, and keep your heart
on the right path. Do not join those who drink too
much wine or gorge themselves on meat, for
drunkards and gluttons become poor, and
drowsiness clothes them in rags.*
—Proverbs 23:19-21

*Who forgives all your sins and heals all your
diseases, who redeems your life from the pit and
crowns you with love and compassion, who
satisfies your desires with good things so that your
youth is renewed like the eagle's.* Psalm 103:3-5

*Who has woe? Who has sorrow? Who has strife?
Who has complaints? Who has needless bruises?
Who has bloodshot eyes? Those who linger over
wine, who go to sample bowls of mixed wine. Do
not gaze at wine when it is red, when it sparkles in
the cup, when it goes down smoothly! In the end it
bites like a snake and poisons like a viper. Your
eyes will see strange sights and your mind
imagine confusing things. You will be like one*

sleeping on the high seas, lying on top of the rigging. "They hit me," you will say, "but I'm not hurt! They beat me, but I don't feel it! When will I wake up so I can find another drink?"
—Proverbs 23:29-35

He heals the brokenhearted and binds up their wounds.—Psalm 147:3

Woe to those who rise early in the morning to run after their drinks, who stay up late at night till they are inflamed with wine.—Isaiah 5:11

The Lord is a refuge for the oppressed, a stronghold in times of trouble. Those who know your name will trust in you, for you, Lord, have never forsaken those who seek you.
—Psalm 9:9-10

Woe to those who are heroes at drinking wine and champions at mixing drinks.—Isaiah 5:22

You have made known to me the path of life; you will fill me with joy in your presence, with eternal pleasures at your right hand.—Psalm 16:11

Let us behave decently, as in the daytime, not in orgies and drunkenness, not in sexual immorality and debauchery, not in dissension and jealously. Rather, clothe yourselves with the Lord Jesus Christ, and do not think about how to gratify the desires of the sinful nature.—Romans 13:13-14

You are forgiving and good, O Lord, abounding in love to all who call to you.—Psalm 86:5

It is better not to eat meat or drink wine or to do anything else that will cause your brother to fall. —
Romans 14:21

For we know that our old self was crucified with him so that the body of sin might be done away with, that we should no longer be slaves to sin because anyone who has died has been freed from sin.—Romans 6:6

Do not get drunk on wine, which leads to debauchery. Instead, be filled with the Spirit.— Ephesians 5:18

*Therefore, there is now no condemnation for those who are in Christ Jesus, because through Christ Jesus the law of the Spirit of life set me free from the law of sin and death. —*Romans 8:1-2

"Be careful, or your hearts will be weighed down with dissipation, drunkenness and the anxieties of life, and that day will close on you unexpectedly like a trap.—Luke 21:34

So whatever you eat or drink or whatever you do,
do it all for the glory of God.
—1 Corinthians 10:31

Since an overseer is entrusted with God's work, he must be blameless—not overbearing, not quick-tempered, not given to drunkenness, not violent, not pursuing dishonest gain.—Titus 1:7

Therefore, since Christ suffered in his body, arm yourselves also with the same attitude, because he who has suffered in his body is done with sin. As a result, he does not live the rest of his earthly life for evil human desires, but rather for the will of God. For you have spent enough time in the past doing what pagans choose to do—living in debauchery, lust, drunkenness, orgies, carousing and detestable idolatry. They think it strange that you do not plunge with them into the same flood of dissipation, and they heap abuse on you. But they will have to give account to him who is ready to judge the living and the dead.—1 Peter 1:1-5

Chapter 10

Resources

Below are some of the many resources I have found so helpful throughout the years to help me escape alcohol prison.

<u>FAVORITE RECOVERY PROGRAMS:</u>

Hola Sober	The Alcohol Experiment
The PATH	Zero Proof Life

<u>FAVORITE PODCASTS:</u>

Beyond the Booze

Cultivate with Kelly Minter

Decidedly Dry

Everything Will Be OK with Dana Perino

Fearless with Cissy Graham Lynch

God Stories with Brad McClendon

Going Beyond Ministries (Priscilla Shirer)

Huberman Lab

InTouch with Dr. Charles Stanley

Jack Hibbs Podcast

Lisa Harper's Back Porch

Livin' the Bream with Shannon Bream

Living Proof with Beth Moore

Proverbs 31 Ministries

Recovery My Way

Rhythms for Life

She Reads Truth

She Surrenders

Sober Gratitudes

Sober Motivation

Sober-Powered

Sobriety Unleashed

The Addiction Connection

The GraceLaced Podcast

The Healthy Christian Women Podcast

The Winning Walk with Pastor Ed Young

Therapy & Theology

This Naked Mind

Tiny Bubbles

Tony Evans' Sermons Podcast

<u>FAVORITE APPS:</u>

HapiBrain

Headspace

Insight Timer

Lived

This Naked Mind Companion

<u>INSTAGRAM:</u>

Affirmations and Quotes

Bubbles of Sobriety

Decidedly Dry

Doc Amen

Drop the Bottle

Jean McCarthy Writes

Life After Alcohol

Naked AF Drinks

Positive Inspirational Quotes

Sober in the City

Sober Humor

Sober Motivation

Sober Powered

Sober Sisters Society

Sober Therapist

Sobriety Activist

Spirit-Led Sobriety22

Spirit Minded Sobriety

The Sober Connection

This Naked Mind

Your Sober Buddy

RECOMMENDED READING:

Addicted to the Monkey Mind: Change the Programming That Sabotages Your Life by J.F. Benoist

A Happier Hour, by Rebecca Weller

Alcohol Explained by William Porter

Alcohol Lied to Me by Craig Beck

A Shepherd Looks at Psalm 23 by W. Phillip Keller

Battlefield of the Mind by Joyce Meyer

Between Breaths: A Memoir of Panic and Addiction, by Elizabeth Vargas (former news anchor)

Blackout: Remembering the Things I Drank to Forget, by Sarah Hepola

Christians and Alcohol: A Scriptural Case for Abstinence by Randy Jaeggli

Cognitive Behavioral Therapy Made Simple: 10 Strategies for Managing Anxiety, Depression, Anger, Panic and Worry by Seth J. Gillihan, PhD

Drink: The Intimate Relationship Between Women and Alcohol, by Ann Downsett Johnson (award-winning journalist and former vice principal at McGill University)

Drink? The New Science of Alcohol and Health by Professor David Nutt

Drinking: A Love Story, by Caroline Knapp

Dry: A Memoir by Augusten Burroughs

Dryland: One Woman's Swim to Sobriety, by Nancy Stearns Bercaw (NCAA All-American swimmer and national champion)

Girl Walks Out of a Bar: A Memoir by Lisa Smith (former attorney)

God Loves the Addict: Experiencing Recovery on the Path of Grace, by Pastor Eddie Snipes

Hardwiring Happiness: The New Brain Science of Contentment, Calm and Confidence by Rick Hanson, PhD

Inside Out by Dr. Larry Crabb (Christian counselor)

Irregular People by Joyce Landorf Heatherley (best-selling Christian author)

It Will Be OK: Trusting God through Fear and Change by Lysa Terkehurst (best-selling Christian speaker and author)

Kick the Drink ... Easily! by Jason Vale

Let it Go!—Breaking Free from Fear and Anxiety by Pastor Tony Evans

Liminal Thinking: Create the Change You Want by Changing the Way You Think by Dave Gray

Lit: A Memoir by M Karr (best-selling author)

Man's Search for Meaning by Viktor E. Frankl, Harold S. Kushner, William J. Winslade

Not Drinking Tonight: A Guide to Creating a Sober Life You Love by Amanda E. White, LPC (founder and director of Therapy for Women Center)

Push Off From Here by Laura McKowen

Quiet: The Power of Introverts in a World That Can't Stop Talking by Susan Cain

RELAPSE: Biblical Prevention Strategies by Dr. Mark Shaw

Resisting Happiness by Matthew Kelly

Seeds of Grace: A Nun's Reflection on the Spirituality of Alcoholics Anonymous by Sister Molly Monahan

Sober Boots: Spiritual Reflections on the Path of Recovery by Heather Kopp (Christian author)

Sober Curious by Ruby Warrington

Sober Mercies: How Love Caught Up With a Christian Drunk by Heather Kopp

Solitude—A Return to the Self by Anthony Storr (psychiatrist and psychoanalyst)

Stop Drinking Now by Allen Carr

Suffering is Never for Nothing by Elisabeth Elliot (Christian missionary)

Temptation—The Battle of Your Life by Pastor Jack Hibbs

The Bible (in particular, Psalms for comfort, and Proverbs for wisdom and understanding)

The Case for Christ by Lee Stroebel (former award-winning legal editor of *The Chicago Tribune,* atheist-turned-Christian, best-selling author)

The Divided Mind: The Epidemic of Mind/Body Disorders by Dr. John Sarno (back pain specialist)

The Drinking Game – How big business, the media and politicians shape the way you drink by Guyon Espiner

The Gifts of Imperfection: Let Go of Who You Think You're Supposed to be and Embrace Who You Are by Brene Brown (professor, lecturer and author)

The Heart of Addiction by Lance Dodes, MD (psychiatrist and psychoanalyst)

The Heart of Addiction: A Biblical Perspective by Dr. Mark Shaw

The Little Book of BIG Change: The No-Willpower Approach to Breaking Any Habit by Amy Johnson, PhD (psychologist, coach, author and speaker)

The Path of Loneliness by Elisabeth Elliot (Christian missionary)

The Power of Habit: Why We Do What We Do in Life and Business by Charles Duhigg (best-selling *New York Times* business reporter

The Power of the Subconscious Mind by Joseph Murphy

The Purpose Driven Life by Pastor Rick Warren

The Relentless Courage of a Scared Child by Tana Amen (psychiatrist and brain health expert)

The Return of the Prodigal Son by Henri J.M. Nouwen (Catholic priest, professor and theologian)

The Sober Diaries: How One Woman Stopped Drinking and Started Living, by Clare Pooley

The Unexpected Joy of Being Sober, by Catherine Gray

The Untethered Soul: The Journey Beyond Yourself by Michael A. Singer (journalist)

This Naked Mind by Annie Grace (best-selling author)

Thirty Days to Overcoming Addiction by Dr. Tony Evans

Unwasted: My Lush Sobriety, by Sacha Z. Scoblic (senior editor, *The Atlantic)*

We are the Luckiest by Laura McKowen (best-selling author)

What Are the Odds? From Crack Addict to CEO by Mike Lindell (founder of My Pillow)

When to Walk Away: Finding Freedom from Toxic People by Pastor Gary Thomas

Why Can't I Drink Like Everyone Else? by Rachel Hart

Why Won't You Apologize? Healing Big Betrayals and Everyday Hurts by Harriet Lerner (psychologist)

Why You Drink and How to Stop by Veronica Valli

Winning the War in Your Mind by Pastor Craig Groeschel

You Just Don't Understand: Women and Men in Conversation by Deborah Tannen, PhD (Professor of Linguistics, Georgetown University)

<u>RECOMMENDED WEBSITES:</u>

https://www.theaddictionconnection.org

https://protectingsobriety.com

https://spiritledsobriety.com

https://thisnakedmind.com

https://zeroprooflife.com

<u>RECOMMENDED YOUTUBE VIDEOS:</u>

"What Alcohol Does to Your Brain and Body" by Dr. Andrew Huberman, Episode 86

"Alcohol Commercial Suddenly Turns Anti-Drinking"

<u>**Epilogue**</u>

Thank you for reading my book. Would you please consider sharing it or sharing information about it with your pastor, family, friends and neighbors and on your social media platforms? While this book was primarily written for my fellow brothers and sisters in Christ—because I think it's high time the subject is talked about openly from the pulpit—the message is for anyone.

Please share a review on Amazon and/or wherever you purchased a copy. I would greatly appreciate it if you would share a screenshot of the cover and a small blurb on your social media platforms to help me get the word out.

The more people who find freedom from alcohol, the sooner alcohol will become like cigarettes: publicly frowned upon and banned from many businesses. No more tormenting ads on TV, in movies, etc. This is the kind of world I hope my grandkids and yours grow up in.

It all starts with us, one soul at a time.

I would be remiss if I didn't encourage my atheist friends, anyone who's angry at God (as I was for years after my dad was murdered), or just allowed themselves to get distracted by the people and things of this world, how to begin or renew a personal relationship with Jesus Christ.

No matter what you've done, how much you've had to drink, no matter HOW bad you think you are—God loves you; He's always loved you, and will always love you. He stands ready to help you turn your life around. All you need to do is ask.

Feel free to contact me or if you'd like to be added to my private online community at:
SpiritLedSobriety@gmail.com.

You're welcome to sign up for my free newsletter at:
https://spiritledsobriety.com

I'd love for you to join my private online community at: https://band.us/band/91347754.

Blessings,

Paulette

Made in the USA
Las Vegas, NV
24 July 2023

75166370R00118